HITLER'S

TIGER I
IN COMBAT

BY BOB CARRUTHERS

Pen & Sword
MILITARY

This edition published in 2013 by
Pen & Sword Military
An imprint of
Pen & Sword Books Ltd
47 Church Street
Barnsley
South Yorkshire
S70 2AS

First published in Great Britain in 2011 in digital format by
Coda Books Ltd.

Copyright © Coda Books Ltd, 2011
Published under licence by Pen & Sword Books Ltd.

ISBN 978 1 78159 129 1

The moral right of Bob Carruthers to be identified as the author of this work has been asserted in accordance with the Copyright, Designs and Patents Act, 1988.

A CIP catalogue record for this book is
available from the British Library

All rights reserved. No part of this book may be reproduced or transmitted in any form or by any means, electronic or mechanical including photocopying, recording or by any information storage and retrieval system, without permission from the Publisher in writing.

Printed and bound by CPI Group (UK) Ltd, Croydon, CR0 4YY

Pen & Sword Books Ltd incorporates the Imprints of Pen & Sword Aviation, Pen & Sword Family History, Pen & Sword Maritime, Pen & Sword Military, Pen & Sword Discovery, Pen & Sword Politics, Pen & Sword Atlas, Pen & Sword Archaeology, Wharncliffe Local History, Wharncliffe True Crime, Wharncliffe Transport, Pen & Sword Select, Pen & Sword Military Classics, Leo Cooper, The Praetorian Press, Claymore Press, Remember When, Seaforth Publishing and Frontline Publishing

For a complete list of Pen & Sword titles please contact
PEN & SWORD BOOKS LIMITED
47 Church Street, Barnsley, South Yorkshire, S70 2AS, England
E-mail: enquiries@pen-and-sword.co.uk
Website: www.pen-and-sword.co.uk

CONTENTS

- INTRODUCTION 4
- PRODUCTION OF THE TIGER 7
- OPERATIONAL STATUS 8
- THE DEVELOPMENT PROCESS.. 11
- THE UNPLEASANT SURPRISE... 13
- DEPLOYMENT 18
- THE MECHANICS OF THE TIGER 1 23
- PRODUCTION HISTORY.. 27
- DESIGN FEATURES... 34
- GETTING TO THE BATTLEFIELD... 38
- MOBILITY... 47
- TIGER RECOVERY 53
- TIGER COLOUR SCHEMES.. 57
- DESIGN REVIEW 59
- PRODUCTION RUN MODIFICATIONS 62
- COMBAT HISTORY 63
- ROAD MARCHES 65
- TACTICAL ORGANISATION 69
- THE RUSSIAN VIEW 71
- TIGER ACES... 74
- TIGERPHOBIA 80
- INSIDE THE TIGER.. 86
- 'YANK' MAGAZINE 89
- TIGER I TANKS IN SICILY... 94
- ARMOUR AND ARMAMENT 99
- THE TWO EXTREMES.. 104
- THE BRITISH RESPONSE 107
- TIGER I TANKS IN NORMANDY.. 108
- THE SOVIET RESPONSE.. 114
- TIGERS IN ITALY 118
- TANK LOSSES 122
- NOTABLE VARIANTS... 123

One of the most famous studies of the Tiger I. This early production model appears to be in almost factory fresh condition.

INTRODUCTION

The Tiger I was the most famous heavy tank used in World War II. It was developed in great haste during 1942 by the Henschel & Sohn company as the answer to the unexpectedly formidable Soviet armour encountered during 1941 in the closing stages of Operation Barbarossa. During that titanic campaign an unpleasant surprise for the German armies appeared in the ominous form of the T-34 and the KV-1 to which the German tank designs of the time could provide no answer. The 50mm calibre high velocity gun of the German Mark III lacked projectile mass and penetrating power while the low velocity gun mounted on the German Mark IV was incapable of penetrating the well sloped armour of the T-34 at anything but the shortest range. The high velocity 88mm anti-aircraft gun, which had been forced into action in an anti-tank role in Russia and the western desert, was the only gun which had demonstrated its effectiveness against even the most heavily armoured ground targets such as The KV1.

Rushed into service in August 1942 the Tiger I design at least gave the Panzerwaffe its first tank capable of mounting the fearsome 88mm gun as its main armament. For the hard pressed men of the Panzewaffe however there was a very high price to pay for the Tiger in both literal and metaphorical terms. The highest price of all, or course, was paid by the slave labourers who were forced to build the Tiger.

The Roman numeral I was only officially added in 1944 when the later Tiger II entered production. The initial official German designation was Panzerkampfwagen VI Ausführung H ('Panzer VI version H'), abbreviated to PzKpfw VI Ausf. H. Somewhat confusingly the tank was redesignated as PzKpfw VI Tiger Ausf. E in March 1943. It also enjoyed the ordnance inventory Sonderkraftzug designation SdKfz 181.

The Tiger I first saw action on 22nd September 1942 near Leningrad. It was not an instant success. Under pressure from Hitler, the tank was driven into action in unfavourable terrain, months earlier than planned. Many early models proved to be mechanically unreliable; in this first action most broke

A Tiger I with the turret number 133 of 1. SS-Pz.-Korps Leibstandarte Adolf Hitler in transit by road march; in the foreground is Schwimmkübel; PK 698.

down. More worryingly two others were easily knocked out by dug-in Soviet anti-tank guns. Of even more concern was the fact that one disabled tank was almost captured intact by the Soviets. It was finally blown up in November 1942 to prevent it falling into Soviet hands. In any event the Soviets used the battlefield experience well and used the time to study the design and begin to prepare a response which, in due course, would emerge as the fearsome Josef Stalin heavy tank which was to prove equal to the Tiger in every respect.

PRODUCTION OF THE TIGER

Production of the Tiger I began in August 1942, and 1,347 were built by August 1944 when production ceased. Production started at a rate of 25 per month and peaked in April 1944 at 104 per month. Battlefield strength peaked at 671 on 1st July 1944. Generally speaking, it took about twice as long to build a Tiger I as any other German tank of the period. However, none of the obvious lessons concerning the need to husband scarce resources were learned and astonishingly when the "improved" model began production in January 1944, the Tiger I was soon phased out in favour of an even more resource hungry monster in the form of the massive, less efficient and even more resource intense Tiger II.

The major problem with the Tiger I was that it simply used too many scarce resources in terms of both manpower and material, especially when compared with the spartan simplicity of the T-34. As a general rule of thumb each the Tiger I cost over twice as much as a Panzer IV and four times as much as a StuG III assault gun. Each Tiger I actually cost 250,000 Reichsmarks as compared to the 103,500 it cost

A rare photograph shows the interior of the Tiger I factory Henschelwerk III at Kassel-Mittelfeld.

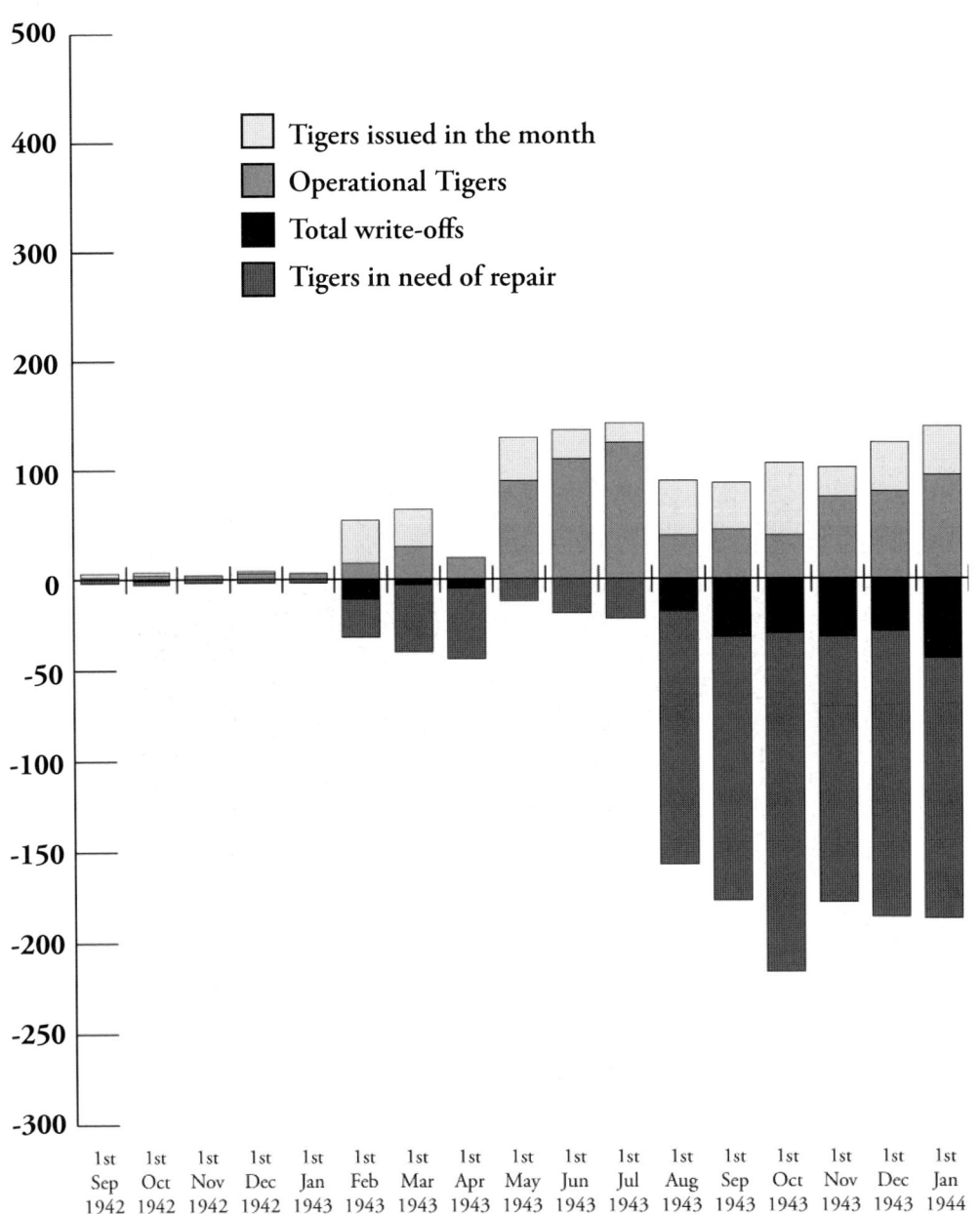

THE EASTERN AND WESTERN FRONTS
TO 5th APRIL 1945

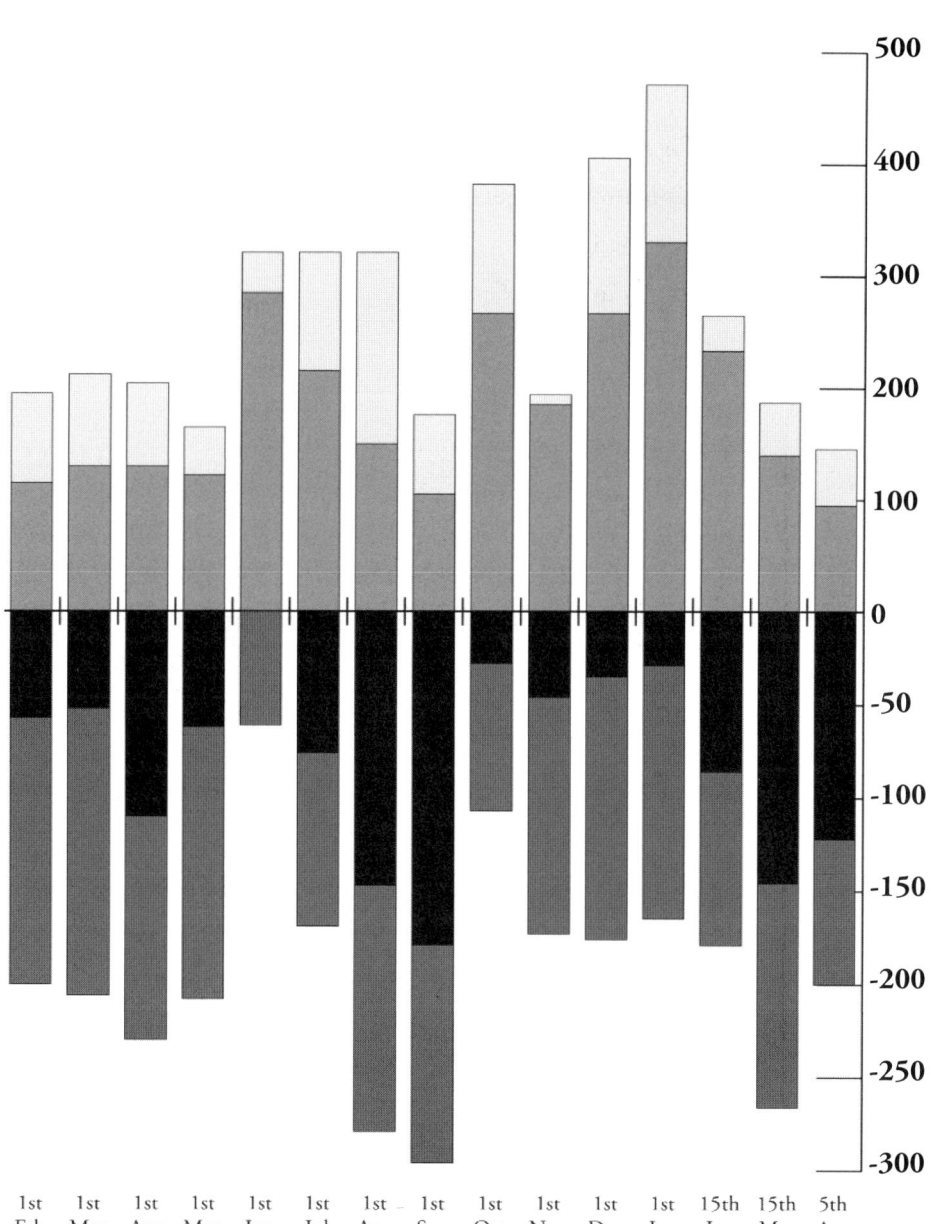

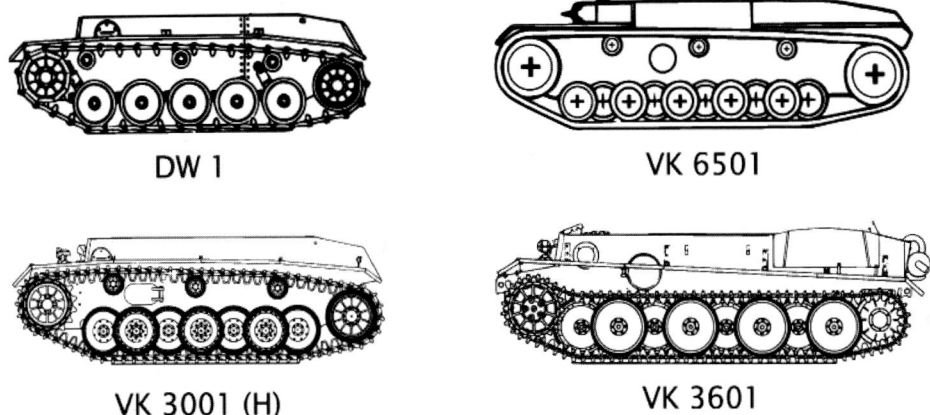

Early development prototype hulls for the Henschel heavy tank programme which ultimately produced the Tiger I.

to manufacture a Panzer IV. The Tiger I was also significantly over engineered which made it difficult to manufacture at a fast rate. The result was an increasing production gap which Speer's hard pressed German tank industry could never hope to close. During the Second World War, over 58,000 American Shermans and 36,000 Soviet T-34s were produced, compared to just 1,347 Tiger I and 492 Tiger II. The closest counterpart to the Tiger from the United States was the M26 Pershing around 200 of which deployed during the war and the Soviet IS-2 of which about 3,800 were built during the war.

The War Office commissioned this illustration on the basis of a photograph from the German newspaper above published in December 1942. Note the lack of muzzle brake on the gun.

THE DEVELOPMENT PROCESS

Henschel & Sohn began development of the vehicle that eventually became the Tiger I in January 1937 when the Waffenamt requested Henschel to develop a *Durchbruchwagen* (breakthrough vehicle) in the 30 metric ton range (see DW 1 hulk opposite). Only one prototype hull was ever built and it never was mounted with a turret. The general configuration and suspension of the Durchbruchwagen prototype in many respects resembled the Panzer III. The proposed turret also bore similarities to existing machines and, had it been completed, it would have greatly resembled the early Panzer IV C turret which sported the short barrelled 7.5cm L/24 cannon.

Before Durchbruchwagen I was completed, however, a new request was issued for a heavier 30 tonne class vehicle with thicker armour; this was known as the Durchbruchwagen II (see VK 6501 opposite). This tank would have carried 50mm of frontal armour and have mounted a Panzer IV turret with the standard 7.5cm L/24 cannon. Overall weight would also have been approximately 36 metric tons. Again only one hull was ever built and a turret was never actually fitted. Development of this vehicle was cancelled in the autumn of 1938 in favour of the more advanced VK3001(H) and VK3601(H) designs. However, both the Durchbruchwagen I and II prototype hulls were used as test vehicles until 1941.

On 9th September 1939, with the invasion of Poland underway, Henschel & Sohn received permission to continue development of a VK3001(H) medium tank

Prototype drawing for the Porsche version of the Tiger I. There were many problems with this design including forward location of the turret made manoevering difficult. There were also many mechanical breakdowns during testing.

and a VK3601(H) heavy tank, both of which apparently pioneered the overlapping and interleaved main road wheel concept as adapted for tank chassis use. Interleaved road wheels were already being used on German military half-tracked vehicles such as the SdKfz 7 although there was very little comparison with regard to the weight of a heavily armoured tank compared to a lightweight half track.

The VK3001(H) was intended be produced in three main variants the first of which was to mount a 7.5cm L/24 low velocity infantry support gun, the second was intended to carry a 7.5cm L/40 dual purpose anti-tank gun, and the third a 10.5cm L/28 artillery piece in a Krupp turret. Overall weight was to be 33 metric tons. The armour was designed to be 50mm on frontal surfaces and 30mm on the side surfaces. Four prototype hulls were completed for testing. Two of these were later used to create the 12.8cm Selbstfahrlafette L/61, also known as Sturer Emil.

The VK3601(H) was intended to weigh 40 metric tons, and carry 100mm of armour on its frontal surfaces, 80mm on turret sides and 60mm on hull sides. The VK3601(H) was also intended to appear in four variants adapted to house a 7.5cm L/24, or a 7.5cm L/43, or a 7.5cm L/70, or a 12.8cm L/28 cannon in a Krupp turret that looked very similar to an enlarged Panzer IVC turret. One prototype hull was built, followed later by five more prototype hulls. The six turrets intended for the prototype hulls were built but never actually fitted and ended their working lives as static defences mounted the Atlantic Wall. The development of the VK3601(H) project was discontinued in early 1942 in favour of the VK4501 project. German combat experience with the French Somua S35 cavalry tank and Char B1 heavy tank, and the British Matilda I and Matilda II infantry tanks in June 1940 showed that the German Army needed better armed and armoured tanks. In 1940 superior tactics had overcome superior enemy armour, but Rommel had endured a nasty shock on the form of a successful British counter attack at Arras. The German tank designers however, took notice of the lessons from the battlefield. Accordingly on 26th May 1941, at an armaments meeting, Henschel and Porsche were asked to submit designs for a 45 tonne heavy tank, to be ready by June 1942. Porsche worked hard and fast to submit an updated version of their VK3001(P) Leopard tank prototype while Henschel worked to develop an improved VK3601(H)tank. Henschel built two prototypes. A VK4501(H) H1 which used the 88mm L/56 cannon and a VK4501(H) H2 which used the 75mm L/70 cannon.

THE UNPLEASANT SURPRISE

On 22 June 1941, Germany launched Operation Barbarossa, the invasion of the Soviet Union. The Germans were shocked to encounter Soviet T-34 medium and KV-1 heavy tanks which completely outclassed anything the Germans were then able to put into the field. The T-34 was almost immune frontally to every gun in German service except the 88mm FlaK 18/36 gun. The Panzer Mark III with the 50mm KwK 38 L/42 main armament could penetrate the sides of a T-34, but had to be very close to do so. To have any chance of penetrating the frontal armour the Panzer III had to close to suicidally short range. The KV-1 was even more heavily armoured and in consequence almost immune to anything but the 88mm FlaK 18/36. The emergence of the Soviet T-34 and KV-1 was a very unpleasant

Dr. Erwin Aders (front row right) was head of Henschel's Tiger I development and construction project and the Tiger's chief designer, tours shop 5 in company with high ranking army officers on September 5th, 1942.

surprise and the shock of the discovery was later recalled by the lead Henschel designer Erwin Aders, *"There was great consternation when it was discovered that the Soviet tanks were superior to anything available to the Heer."* In the scramble to come up with an strong defensive alternative to the Russian armour an immediate weight increase to 45 tonnes and an increase in gun calibre to 88mm was ordered. The due date for new prototypes was brought forward to 20th April 1942, Adolf Hitler's birthday.

Porsche and Henschel submitted prototype designs, Tiger (P) and Tiger (H), and they were put through their paces at Rastenburg before Hitler. The Henschel design was accepted as the best overall design. The Porsche gasoline-electric hybrid power unit performed poorly on the day with frequent breakdowns. It also used large quantities of copper, a strategic war material which was in very short supply. The contract was duly awarded to Henschel & Sohn.

Unlike the later Panther tank however, the designs for the Tiger did not incorporate any of the design innovations incorporated into the T-34: the defensive benefits of sloping armour and the corresponding saving in terms of weight were absent from both the Henschel and the Porsche designs, with the thickness and weight of the

A newly completed Tiger is lowered on to a railway carriage ready to commence its journey to the front.

Tiger's armour making up for this oversight.

With the contract in the bag there was no time to loose and Henschel began production of the Panzerkampfwagen VI Ausf. H in August 1942 at its tank factory Henschelwerk III in Kassel-Mittelfeld.

The official designation from March 1943 onwards was Panzerkampfwagen VI SdKfz 181 Tiger Ausf E until Hitler's order, dated February 27th, 1944, abolished the designation Panzerkampfwagen VI and ratified the use of the new designation Panzerkampfwagen Tiger Ausf. E. This was to remain the official designation until the end of the war. For common use the name was frequently shortened to Tiger - the name purportedly given to the machine by its frustrated rival designer Ferdinand Porsche.

The firm of Henschel & Sohn was established in the early 1800s as a builder of locomotives and it was only during World War I that the firm undertook the business of armament manufacturing for the first time. The company kept up the new operations during the inter-war years and by the time Hitler was ready to re-arm Germany Henschel was ready and waiting to oblige. By the time of the second World War, the company was producing locomotives, tanks, diesel engines, trucks, aeroplanes and artillery pieces. Henschel manufactured all of the main battle tank types with the exception of the Panzer IV. This meant that at various times the Panzer I, II and III as well as the Panther, Tiger I and Tiger II all rolled off the Henschel production lines.

The firm of Henschel & Sohn incorporated three huge engineering works in and around Kassel. Werk I in Kassel was devoted to locomotive assembly and gun production, Werk II in the Rothenditmold area consisted of a large foundry, boiler and other locomotive component shops and Werk III in Mittelfeld was primarily devoted to tank assembly and component manufacture.

The Mittelfeld Werkes were situated on both sides of a railway line running north to south. Looking south, those buildings on the right side of the railway line were used for manufacturing locomotive components and truck and engine repair. The main storage area for tank components was also on the right side of the track including sheds that held Tiger hulls and turrets. On the right side of the track were 4 main shops numbered 1, 2, 3 and 5. (Shop 4 was planned but never built.). Tiger manufacturing took place in shops 3 and 5.

At its peak the factory employed a total of over 8000 workers for tank production. Sadly, extensive use was made of slave labour and the victims were treated abominably being effectively worked to death. The Henschel works were in production round the clock seven days a week. The labour force, both slave labourers and willing workers performed two exhausting 12 hour shifts but the night shift for a variety of reasons produced only 50% of the output of the day shift.

A manufacturing process known as the *"takte"* system was used in the assembly shops. That system relied on a timed rhythm for each step in the manufacturing process. There were nine steps or *takte* used in manufacturing the Tiger I. In surviving factory photos the reader should note the takte signs on the shop wall denoting which step is being performed in that location.

Each *takte* took six hours. The total time to complete a Tiger, including the various machining processes, was estimated to be 14 days and incorporated 300,000 man hours. An average of 18 to 22 tanks were carried at any one time in the hull assembly line and approximately ten tanks were carried in the final assembly line.

The first 4 *takte* revolved around hull machining and preparation. Henschel itself did not have the capability to weld or bend the massive heavy armour plates used in the Tiger and actually received the raw hulls and turrets from sub contractors. The turrets were manufactured by Wegmann und Company, which was conveniently also located in Kassel. The raw hulls were manufactured by two firms, Krupp and Dortmund-Hoerder Huettenverein. The hull processing steps all took place in shop 3.

A particularly fine study of a Tiger I in profile.

THE CONTEMPORARY VIEW NO. 1
NEW GERMAN TANKS
Extracted from
Technical and Tactical Trends no. 18, 1943

Several new types of German tanks have been reported to be in existence:

a) Mark I (C) - No details are known but it is probable that this is a redesigned Mark I intended for airborne or landing operations. The original Mark I tank weighed about 6 tons.

b) Mark II Special - The original Mark II tank (weight about 9 tons) has for some time been considered obsolescent as a combat tank. The new tank probably has thicker armour and a more powerful engine. One of the most important features is that it is reportedly armed with the long-barrelled 50mm gun which is used in the new Mark III tanks. The result should be a comparatively light, fast tank with adequate striking power, probably suitable for use as a tank destroyer.

c) Mark VI - This is a heavy tank. No details other than the actual nomenclature are known, but it seems probable that this model is an entirely new departure in German tank design. It has been anticipated for some time that the Marks III and IV might be superseded by a new type incorporating the best features of each model and introducing features borrowed from British and possibly American designs. Having obtained a tank gun of first quality in the long-barrelled 75mm tank gun (40), the weapon mounted in the new Mark IV tanks, it is probable that this weapon or an 88mm weapon is the principal armament. The basic armour may be as thick as 80 or 100mm, and spaced armour, at least in front, is probably incorporated. There may also be skirting armour. Face-hardened armour is probably used, and the speed is not expected to be under 25mph.

Reports of a German heavy tank have been received over a considerable period of time. Apparently the most recent is the statement of a German captured in Tunisia. According to the prisoner, he belonged to an independent heavy tank battalion, which consisted of a headquarters company and two armoured companies. Each armoured company was equipped with nine 50 ton tanks. The tanks were armed with 88mm guns and were capable of a speed of 50 kilometers (about 30 miles) an hour. Whether or not this is the Mark VI tank is not known.

DEPLOYMENT

Besides Russia, the Tiger was also deployed in Tunisia as it was this theatre which gave the western allies their first glimpse of the tank in the field. Prior to the arrival of the Tiger in Tunisia allied intelligence had been forced to rely on carefully placed German newspaper stories and limited intelligence provided by the Soviets. The first widely circulated intelligence report (see page 17) appeared in the US army intelligence publication entitled *Tactical and Technical Trends No. 18* which was published on 11th February 1943 some five months after the Tiger had first appeared in combat in Russia. It is interesting to note that the name Tiger had not yet come to be associated with the tank.

As the Tunisian campaign developed, Tiger tanks began appear more frequently on the battlefield albeit in limited numbers. However, their heavy armour and powerful armament allowed them dominate the initial tank battles fought in the open terrain of North Africa, but their mechanical unreliability and

A Tiger I deployed in Tunisia. Note the bemused locals to the right.

The Tiger was deployed late in August 1942 but first saw action on 22nd September 1942. The machines were operating in the Army Group North sector near Lenningrad where the terrain was marshy and entirely unsuited to a colossus such as the Tiger I. This rare photograph gives a vivid impression of the type of terrain which the first Tigers were expected to traverse.

lack of numbers meant that they were never to be massed in great numbers and that they served in a primarily supporting role.

The following pages feature a further U.S. intelligence report describing the German Tiger tank originally appeared in *Tactical and Technical Trends*, No. 20 on 11th March 1943. By this time, accurate information on the Tiger tank was starting to be received from destroyed remnants of Tigers captured by the British forces in Tunisia. This is the second glimpse of how allied intelligence reported the arrival of the Tiger on the battlefield. At this stage the name Tiger was still not in use and the Americans did not use the Roman numerals with the new machine being simply refereed to as the PZ.KW. 6

THE CONTEMPORARY VIEW NO.2
GERMAN HEAVY TANK IN ACTION IN TUNISIA

As reported in the press and as previously indicated in Tactical and Technical Trends (No. 18, p.6) a German heavy tank has been in action in Tunisia. So far as can be definitely determined, this is the first time the Germans have used a heavy tank in combat. Whether or not it is the Pz.Kw. 6 cannot be definitely stated. At least one heavy tank has been captured, and while complete details are not yet available, there is sufficient reasonably confirmed data to warrant at least a partial tentative description at this time.

The chief features of this tank are the 88mm gun, 4-inch frontal armour, heavy weight, and lack of spaced armour. The accompanying sketch roughly indicates the appearance of the tank, but should not be accepted as wholly accurate.

The tank has a crew of 5. It is about 20 feet long, 12 feet wide, and 9 $\frac{1}{2}$ feet high. The gun overhangs the nose by almost 7 feet. It is reported that the weight is 56 tons or, with modifications, as much as 62 tons.

The power unit is a single 12-cylinder engine. A speed of at least 20 mph can be achieved. Two types of track are thought to exist: an operational track 2 feet 4.5 inches wide, and a loading track which is just under 2 feet. The suspension system consists of a front driving sprocket, a small rear idler, and 24 Christie-type wheels on each side giving it an appearance similar to the familiar German half-track suspension system. There are 8 axles.

There is no armour skirting for protection of the suspension. The armour plating is as follows:

Lower nose plate	62mm (2.4 in)	60° inwards
Upper nose plate	102mm (4 in)	20° inwards
Front plate	62mm (2.4 in)	80° outwards
Driver plate	102mm (4 in)	10° outwards

Turret sides and rear	82mm (3.2 in)	Vertical
Lower sides (behind bogies)	62mm (2.4 in)	Vertical
Upper sides	82mm (3.2 in)	Vertical
Rear	82mm (3.2 in)	20° inwards
Floor	26mm	(1 in)
Top	26mm	(1 in)

The turret front and mantlet range in thickness between a minimum of 97mm (3.8 in) to a (possible) maximum of 200mm (7.9 in). It appears that the armour is not face-hardened.

The armament of the tank consists of an 88mm gun and two 7.92mm (.315-in) machine guns. The 88mm has a double-baffle muzzle brake and fires the same fixed ammunition as the usual 88mm AA/AT gun. As already indicated, the gun overhangs the nose of the tank by almost 7 feet. The turret rotates through 360 degrees and is probably power-operated. Three smoke-generator dischargers are located on each side of the turret.

COMMENT

From the above characteristics, it is apparent that the Pz.Kw. 6 is designed to be larger and more powerful than the Pz.Kw. 4. As far as known, a Pz.Kw. 5 tank has not been used in combat. The noteworthy differences between the Pz.Kw. 4 and Pz.Kw. 6 are as follows:

Armour	Pz.Kw. 4	Pz.Kw. 6
Minimum	20mm	26mm
Maximum	50 to 80mm*	102mm**
Principal Armament	75mm (long-barrelled gun)	88mm (AA/AT gun)

A 360-degree rotating turret is used in both the Pz.Kw. 6 and Pz.Kw. 4.

The appearance of the Pz.Kw. 6 indicates that the Germans continue to see the need for a fully armoured vehicle equipped with a weapon capable of dealing with hostile tanks as well as with other targets that might hold up the advance of attacking elements.

This tank is undoubtedly an effective weapon, but not necessarily formidable.

In the first place, a vehicle weighing from 56 to 62 tons presents many difficult logistical problems. Also, it is reported that one heavy tank was destroyed by a British six-pounder (57mm) antitank gun at a range of about 500 yards; out of 20 rounds fired, 5 penetrated the tank, 1 piercing the side of the turret and coming out the other side, and another penetrating an upper side plate at an angle of impact of about 15 degrees.

*Attained by attaching extra armour plate to protect critical points on the tank.
**Basic armour plate. The turret front and mantlet may possibly be 200mm thick.

A Tiger I deployed to supplement the Afrika Korps operating in Tunisia, January 1943.

THE MECHANICS OF THE TIGER I

The Tiger was essentially at the prototype stage when it was first hurried into service, and therefore changes both small and large were made throughout the production run. A redesigned turret with a lower, less bulky commander's cupola was the most significant early change. To cut costs, the submersion capability was reduced and an external air-filtration system was dropped.

The rear of the tank held an engine compartment flanked by two floodable rear compartments each containing a fuel tank, radiator, and fans. German industry had not developed an adequate heavy diesel engine, so a fuel hungry petrol power plant had to be used. The initial engine was a 21 litre (1282 cu. in.) 12 cylinder Maybach HL 210 P45 with 650 PS (641hp, 478kW). Although a good and reliable engine, it was inadequate for the size and weight vehicle. From the 250th production Tiger Chassis 250251, this engine was replaced by the updated HL 230 P45 (23 litres/1410 cu. in.) with 700 PS (690hp, 515kW). The engine was in V-form, with two cylinder banks at 60 degrees. An inertial starter was mounted on its right side, driven via chain gears through a port in the rear wall. The engine could be lifted out through a hatch on the hull roof. The engine drove two front sprockets, which were mounted low to the ground.

The eleven-tonne turret had a hydraulic motor the drive for which was powered by mechanical drive from the engine. Rotation was slow and took about a minute to swing through 360°. The suspension used sixteen torsion bars, with eight suspension arms per side. To save space, the swing arms were leading on one side and trailing on the other. There were three road wheels on each arm, giving a good cross-country ride. However the smoothness of the ride was bought at a high price. The constant need to remove the front road wheels in order to gain access to the rear wheels was to become the bane of Tiger I crews from day one.

The problem from the crew's point of view was that the heavy wheels which had a diameter of 800mm (31 in) were overlapped and interleaved. Removing one inner wheel that had lost its tyre, which was a fairly common occurrence, could therefore require the removal of up to nine outer wheels. This was bad enough

The cumbersome road wheel assembly of the Tiger I can be clearly seen in this photograph taken at the Henschel works. It is easy to understand why these wheels could become jammed solid with mud, ice or snow requiring huge efforts to repair.

under calm conditions but it meant there was no way of making a fast change in the combat zone and many precious Tigers were blown up which could otherwise have been saved. The wheels could also become packed with mud or snow that could then freeze. Eventually, a new 'steel' wheel design, closely resembling those on the Tiger II, with an internal tire was substituted, and which like the Tiger II, were only overlapped, and not interleaved.

Another new feature which was to cause problems was the untested Maybach-Olvar hydraulically-controlled pre-selector gearbox and semi-automatic transmission. The extreme weight of the tank also required a new steering system. Instead of the clutch-and-brake designs of lighter vehicles, a variation on the tested and proven British Merritt-Brown single radius system was used. The Tiger I, like all German tanks, used regenerative steering which was hydraulically operated - the separate tracks could therefore be turned in opposite directions at the same time, so the Tiger I could pivot in place, and completely turn around in a distance of only 3.44 meters (11.28 ft.). Since the vehicle had an eight-speed gearbox, it thus had sixteen different radii of turn. If an even smaller radius was needed, the tank could be turned by using brakes. There was an actual steering wheel and the steering system at least was robust, reliable, easy to use and ahead of its time. The British T. I. Summary No. 104 was issued on 16th May 1943 gave the British troops in the field a pretty accurate summary of the type of tank they were facing.

An extract from the Tigerfibel, the commander's manual: "If you travel 7km, your wide tracks will throw up the dust from 1 hectare of land. You will be recognised from far away and will lose your most efective weapon - surprise."

During action the laborious process of re-fuelling and re-arming the Tiger I was a never ending task for the hard pressed crew members.

PRODUCTION HISTORY

While the Tiger I was justifiably feared by many of its opponents, it was also over-engineered, used expensive labour intensive materials and production methods, and was time-consuming to produce. Despite its lasting reputation the tank was actually produced in relatively small numbers. Only 1,347 were built between August 1942 and August 1944 when production ceased. Throughout its brief life the Tiger I was particularly prone to certain types of track failures and immobilisations, it was unreliable mechanically reliable and ferociously expensive to maintain and complicated to transport. Due to its wide tracks powered by interlocking and over lapping road wheels the Tiger I required that a total of eight road wheels consisting of the outer four road wheels on both of the vehicle were to be removed if it was to be transported by rail.

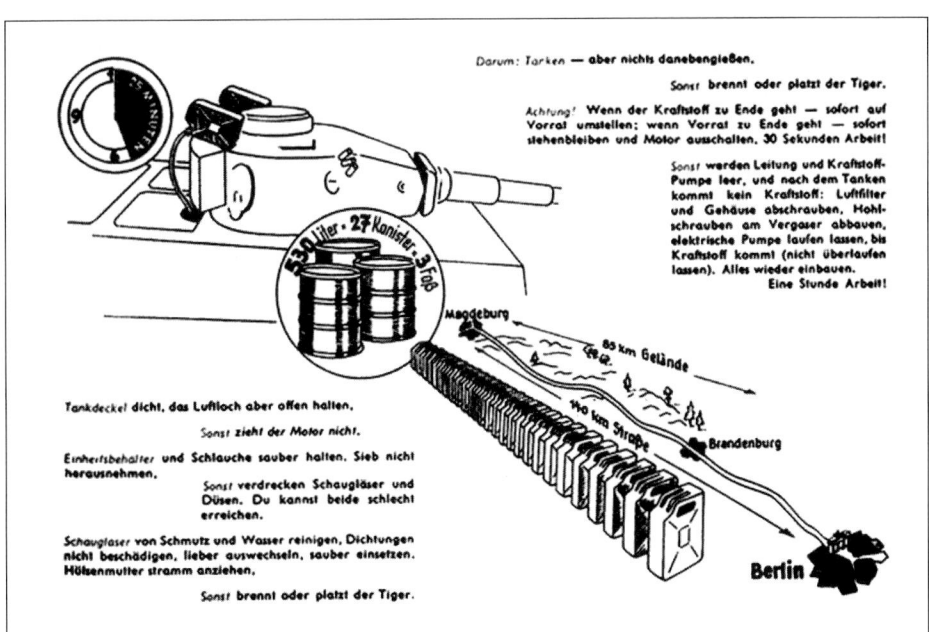

The humorous instruction manual for the tank, the Tigerfibel, was somewhat unorthodox by Third Reich standards. Full of risque sketches and irreverant statements, this is one of the more conventional pages which compares the tank's cross country capability against a road march.

THE CONTEMPORARY VIEW NO.3
Pz. Kw. VI

" The following additional information on the Pz. Kw. VI has been collated from captured documents and reports from Russian and North Africa:

(a) The tank can be submerged to a depth of up to 16ft for fording rivers and other water obstacles. Further information on this development is contained at Appendix C.

(b) An automatic fire extinguisher is provided. Heat-sensitive elements are arranged in suitable positions in the engine compartment. If fire breaks out, one of these elements will cause an electric circuit to operate the extinguisher which will there upon discharge a fire-extinguishing agent for a period of seven seconds. If the fire is severe, the circuit will remain closed and the process will be repeated one or more times until either the fire is put out or the reservoir of the fire extinguisher is exhausted. The reservoir holds 9lbs of extinguishing agent.

(c) The gearbox is preselective and is cooled by a fan which also cools the manifold.

(d) Standard German petrol with an octane number of 74 or 78 is used for the engine.

(e) Reference summary 102, appendix D, North Africa now reports that the total amount of 8.8cm ammunition carried is 92 rounds stowed in racks and bins, 46 rounds each side of the tank.

(f) It is confirmed that the 8.8cm tank gun is electrically fired. "

(g) Oil capacities are as follows:

Engine	28 litres (6.2 galls)
Gearbox & steering units (common sump)	32 litres (7 galls)
Final drive units	8 litres (14 pints)
Turret traversing gear	5 litres (8.75 pints)
Fan drive	6 litres (10.5 pints)

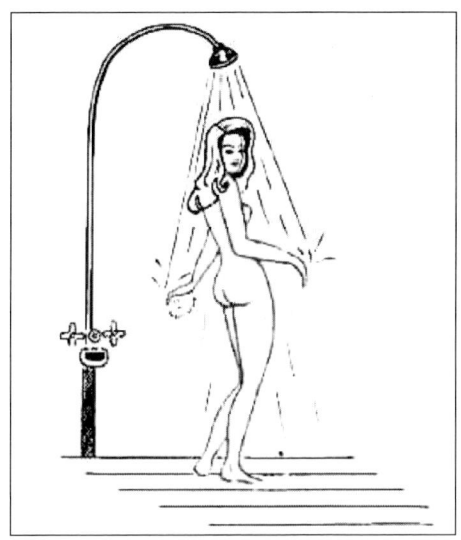

A typical risque illustration from Tigerfibel: "Like a fresh shower, the water flushes through the case and removes the heat accrued by combustion and friction, taking it to the radiators."

The other huge drawback of the Tiger was the enormous fuel consumption associated with such a heavy vehicle. The 1943 log book a captured Tiger circulated by the British M.I.10 intelligence unit which gives a fascinating insight into the fuel consumption characteristics of the Tiger I. The British report is shown overleaf on page 30.

With the conclusion of the Tunisian campaign there was adequate time to study the battlefield results achieved by the Tiger. Captured vehicles provided a wealth of accurate technical information A far more detailed account of the Tiger in combat was reported by the US army intelligence service in their monthly update for June 1943 which refers to the vehicle, for the first time, as the "Tiger". This US report appears on page 31.

During the course of the war, the Tiger I saw combat on the three main German battlefronts. It was usually deployed in independent tank battalions, which on occasion proved to be extremely formidable. In the right hands the Tiger I could be relied upon to turn some spectacularly one sided tactical situations in favour of the hard pressed men of the Heer. At the operational level however, there were never enough Tigers to affect the outcome of a major battle. In the tactical arena the Tiger I demanded good handling by experienced crews who knew and respected the limitations of the machine. Even with the very best crews it was soon apparent that the Tiger I was by no means a miracle weapon. It was always vulnerable to regular battlefield weapons such as the British 6 pounder which could prove deadly if the Tiger I was within range as this account from the US intelligence briefing update *Tactical and Technical Trends* reproduced on page 22 clearly demonstrates. American reports tended to favour the use of the Arabic numeral 6 as opposed to the German designated VI.

THE CONTEMPORARY VIEW NO.4
NOTE ON ENTRIES IN LOG BOOK OF PZ.KW.VI (H)

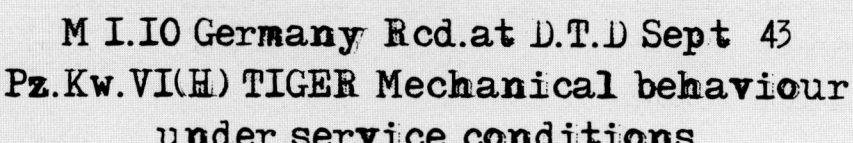

M I.10 Germany Rcd.at D.T.D Sept 43
Pz.Kw.VI(H) TIGER Mechanical behaviour under service conditions

"Entries show that 4917 litres of petrol went into the fuel tanks of this vehicle during a period in which 489km were covered. In other words the apparent petrol consumption was over 10 litres per km. Even if it is assumed that the tanks (total capacity 530 litres) were empty at the start and full at the finish, the consumption would still work out at about 9 litres per km.

These figures are higher than the petrol consumption quoted in the official German specs, viz:

Roads	4.5 litres per km	1.58 galls per mile
Cross Country	7.8 litres per km	2.76 galls per mile

The following additional points have been noted in the log book:

120 km - Log started
136 km - Wireless Tested
160 km - Test run by workshops company
200 km - Wireless Tested/Engine oil and air cleaner oil
343 km - New gearbox fitted
365 km - Tooth sprocket ring (offside sprocket) changed
482 km - New engine & new nearside fan drive clutch fitted
609 km - Log closes"

THE CONTEMPORARY VIEW NO.5
NEW GERMAN HEAVY TANK

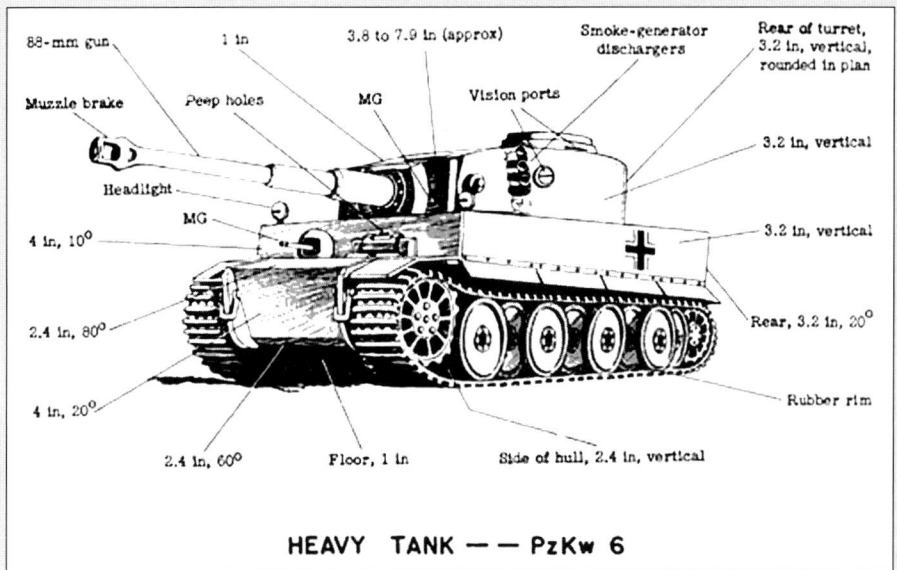

HEAVY TANK — — PzKw 6

In Tunisia the German Army sent into combat, apparently for the first time, its new heavy tank, the Pz. Kw. 6, which it calls the "Tiger". The new tank's most notable features are its 88mm gun, 4-inch frontal armour, great weight, and lack of spaced armour. Although the Pz. Kw. 6 has probably been adopted as a standard German tank, future modifications may be expected.

The "Tiger" tank, which is larger and more powerful than the Pz. Kw. 4,1 is about 20 feet long, 12 feet wide, and 9 ½ feet high. The barrel of the 88mm gun overhangs the nose by almost 7 feet. The tank weighs 56 tons in action (or, with certain alterations, as much as 62 tons), and is reported to have a maximum speed of about 20 miles per hour. It normally has a crew of five.

The armament of the Pz. Kw. 6 consists of the 88mm tank gun (Kw. K. 36), which fires fixed ammunition similar to, or identical with, ammunition for the usual 88mm antiaircraft-antitank gun; a 7.92mm machine gun (MG

34) which is mounted coaxially on the left side of the 88mm; and a second 7.92mm machine gun (MG 34) which is hull-mounted and fires forward.

In addition, a set of three smoke-generator dischargers is carried on each side of the turret.

The turret rotates through 360 degrees, and the mounting for the gun and coaxial machine gun appears to be of the customary German type.

The suspension system, which is unusually interesting, is illustrated in figure 4. The track is made of metal. To the far right in figure 4 is the front-drive sprocket and to the far left the rear idler. There are no return rollers, since the track rides on top of the Christie-type wheels, which are rubber rimmed. It will be noted that there are eight axles, each with three wheels to a side, or each with one single and one double wheel to a side. There are thus 24 wheels - 8 single wheels and 8 double wheels on each side of the tank. The system of overlapping is similar to the suspension system used on German half-tracks.

The tank is provided with two tracks, a wide one (2 feet, 4.5 inches) and a narrow one (just under 2 feet). The wide track is the one used in battle, the narrow being for administrative marches and where manoeuvrability and economy of operation take precedence over ground pressure. The dotted line in figure 4 indicates the outer edge of the narrow track. When the narrow track is used, the eight wheels outside the dotted line can be removed.

The armour plating of the Pz. Kw. 6 has the following thicknesses and angles:

Lower nose plate	62mm (24 in)	60° inwards
Upper nose plate	102mm (4 in)	20° inwards
Front plate	62mm (24 in)	80° outwards
Driver plate	102mm (4 in)	10° outwards
Turret front and mantlet	Up to 200mm (8 in)	Rounded
Turret sides and rear	82mm (3.2 in)	Vertical
Lower sides (behind bogies)	60mm (24 in)	Vertical
Upper sides	82mm (3.2 in)	Vertical

Rear	82mm (3.2 in)	20° inwards
Floor	26mm (1 in)	
Top	26mm (1 in)	

The angular (as opposed to rounded) arrangement of most of the armour is a bad design feature; reliance seems to be placed on the quality and thickness of the armour, with no effort having been made to present difficult angles of impact. In addition, none of the armour is face-hardened. The familiar German practice of increasing a tank's frontal armour at the expense of the side armour is also apparent in the case of the Pz. Kw. 6.

Undoubtedly the Germans developed the "Tiger" tank to meet the need for a fully armoured vehicle equipped with a heavy weapon capable of dealing with a variety of targets, including hostile tanks. Although the "Tiger" can perform these duties, its weight and size make it a logistical headache. It is entirely probable that the Germans, realizing this disadvantage, are continuing to develop tanks in the 30-ton class. Further, it is interesting to note that the Pz. Kw. 6 has proved vulnerable to the British 6-pounder (57mm) antitank gun when fired at a range of about 500 yards.

A Tiger captured by Allied Forces near Tunis, 1943. It was vehicles such as this which allowed the Allies to unlock the secrets of the Tiger I.

DESIGN FEATURES

The Tiger I differed from earlier German tanks principally in its design philosophy. Its predecessors all sought balance mobility, armour and firepower, and as a result were being outgunned by their opponents. The Tiger I represented a brand new approach which emphasised firepower and armour at the expense of mobility. Nonetheless the new heavy tank was surprisingly sprightly and was not that much slower than the best of its opponents. However, with over 50 metric tons dead weight, suspensions, gearboxes and other vital items had clearly reached their design limits and as a result Tiger I breakdowns were infuriatingly frequent.

Design studies for a new heavy tank had actually been started in 1937, but had stalled long before production planning stage was reached. Renewed impetus for the Tiger was provided by the discovery of outstanding battlefield qualities of the Soviet T-34 encountered in 1941. Although the general design and layout were broadly similar to the previous medium tank, the Panzer IV, the Tiger weighed more than twice as much. This was due to its substantially thicker armour, the larger main gun, greater volume of fuel and ammunition storage, larger engine, and more solidly-built transmission and suspension. Unfortunately for the Panzerwaffe not all of the lessons from the T-34 were absorbed. Sloping angular armour deflects most shots away from the vehicle and can therefore afford to be thinner and lighter. The Armour plates on the Tiger were mostly flat, with interlocking construction however the armour joints were of high quality, being stepped and welded rather than riveted which overcame one of the main disadvantages of riveted construction found in many allied tanks of the early war period.

The nominal armour of the Tiger at its thickest point on the gun mantlet was 200mm and an unprecedented 120mm thick on most of the mantlet. The Tiger I had frontal hull armour 100mm (3.9in) thick and frontal turret armour of 120mm (4.7in), as opposed to the 80mm (3.1in) frontal hull and 50mm (2 in) frontal turret armour of contemporary models of the Panzer IV. It also had 60mm (2.4in) thick hull side plates and 80mm armour on the side superstructure and rear, turret sides and rear was 80mm. The top and bottom armour was 25mm

(1in) thick; from March 1944, the turret roof was thickened to 40mm (1.6in).

The gun's breech and firing mechanism were derived from the famous German "88" dual purpose flak gun, the Flugabwehr-kanone. The 88mm Kampfwagonkanone 36 L/56 gun was the variant developed for the Tiger and was the most effective and feared tank guns of World War II. The Tiger's gun had a very flat trajectory and extremely accurate Leitz Turmzielfernrohr TZF 9b sights (later replaced by the monocular TZF 9c). In British wartime firing trials, five successive hits were scored on a 16 by 18 inch (410 by 460mm) target at a range of 1,200 yards (1,100m). Tigers were reported to have knocked out enemy tanks at ranges greater than 2.5 miles (4,000m), although most World War II engagements were fought at much shorter ranges.

Ammunition types :
  i) 8.8 cm KwK 36# Ammunition (General Issue)
  ii) PzGr.39 (Armour Piercing Capped Ballistic Cap)
  iii) PzGr.40 (Armour Piercing Composite Rigid)
  iv) Hl. Gr.39 (High Explosive Anti-Tank)
  v) Sch Sprgr. Patr. L/4.5 (Incendiary Shrapnel)

The 88mm ammunition carried by the Tiger I was exceptionally bulky and an ingenious array of stowage solutions were incorporated which allowed the tank to accommodate up to 100, and sometimes more, of these space consuming rounds.

THE CONTEMPORARY VIEW NO.6
ATTACK AGAINST GERMAN HEAVY TANK Pz. Kw. 6

"The following report by an observer on the Tunisian front furnishes some comments as a guide to training in antitank action against this tank.

It appears that the first of these tanks to be destroyed in this theatre were accounted for by British 6-pounders (57mm). An account of this action, as reported by a British Army Officer, follows:

"The emplaced 6-pounders opened fire at an initial range of 680 yards. The first rounds hit the upper side of the tank at very acute angles and merely nicked the armour. As the tank moved nearer, it turned in such a manner that the third and fourth shots gouged out scallops of armour, the fifth shot went almost through and the next three rounds penetrated completely and stopped the tank. The first complete penetration was at a range of 800 yards, at an angle of impact of 30 degrees from normal, through homogeneous armour 82mm (approximately 3 1/3 inches) thick. Ammunition used was the 57mm semi-AP solid shot.

"One element of this action contains an important lesson that should be brought to the attention of all AT elements and particularly tank destroyer units."

(a) "The British gunners did not open until the enemy tank was well within effective range."

(b) "In addition to opening fire with the primary weapon - the 57mm - the AT unit also opened with intense light machine-gun fire which forced the tank to button up and in effect blinded him. His vision apparently became confused and he was actually traversing his gun away from the AT guns when he was knocked out for good.

(c) "Once they opened fire, the British gunners really poured it on and knocked out one more heavy tank and six Pz. Kw. 3s. Also, for good measure, one armoured car."

The conclusions to be drawn from this action, according to the British officer quoted, are:

(a) "The unobstructed vision of the gunner in a tank destroyer gives him a very real advantage over his opponent squinting through the periscope or narrow vision slits of a tank.

(b) "The tank destroyer unit must force the enemy tank to 'button up' by intense fire from every weapon he has, including machine-guns, tommy guns, and rifles."

The size and weight of a tank such as the Pz. Kw. 6 present many problems. It has been indicated from unofficial enemy sources that extensive reconnaissance of terrain, bridges, etc., was necessary before operations with this tank could be undertaken. Bridges have to be reinforced in many cases, and soil conditions must be good for its effective operation. It can therefore be assumed that its field of operation is limited.

Reports so far indicate that the use of this tank is chiefly to support other armoured units, including employment as mobile artillery. As a support tank it is always in rear of lighter units. In one reported skirmish in Tunisia, the lighter units formed the spear-head; as soon as enemy tanks were decoyed into range the lighter tanks fanned out, leaving the heavier tanks in the rear to engage the enemy units.

The Pz. Kw. 6 is now considered a standard German tank. Present production figures are believed to be at a maximum of 800 per month.

A tank commander confers with supporting infantry from the Waffen-SS. This shot was taken in the summer of 1943.

GETTING TO THE BATTLEFIELD

The problems of moving the Tiger tank from place to place were significant and were especially marked in relation to rail movement by rail. The Tiger's width placed the vehicle at the very limits of the abilities of Europe's rail systems to cope with the vehicle and special transit tracks had to be developed if the tanks were to be moved at all. In order to support the considerable weight of the Tiger, the tracks were an unprecedented 725mm (28.5in) wide. Which was too wide to be carried by rail. To meet rail-freight size restrictions, the outer row of wheels had to be removed and special 520mm (20in) wide transport tracks installed. With a good crew, a track change took 20 minutes. British intelligence was bolstered by the 1944 interrogation of a POW who had experience of the enormous difficulties entailed in moving the Tiger by rail.

Another early U.S. report on the German heavy Tiger tank, Pz. Kw. 6 was featured in *Tactical and Technical Trends*, 6th May 1943 while the Tunisian campaign was coming to a close. By now the Tiger I was becoming increasingly familiar on the battlefields and as a result the intelligence reports were increasingly accurate.

As German prisoners began to be taken in Tunisia so the knowledge available to the allies increased. *Notes On Tank Tactics* was derived from interrogations of these prisoners and was published in April 1943 by the R.A.C. liaison unit. By this stage more and more detail was beginning to emerge on the exact statistical role in which the Tiger I was employed in Tunisia.

The first reports of the Tiger I in combat in Tunisia had actually begun to filter in from January 1943. From the speed at which the German battlefield tactics were altered it appears fairly clear that the German tank crews were quickly disabused of the notion that the new tank was invincible. The Tiger I was without a doubt a strongly built tank with many superior attributes, but it could be easily destroyed by regular battlefield weaponry, especially if the crew were not constantly vigilant for attacks from the rear or the side. This further extract from a British intelligence report from M.I.10 dated September 1943 underlines the fact that the British were fast learning the weaknesses of the Tiger in action.

Routine maintenance of the Tiger I was incredibly difficult and required a mobile crane as it was necessary to remove the turret in order to change the gear box. This was a frustratingly frequent occurrence.

THE CONTEMPORARY VIEW NO.7
PRISONER OF WAR DESCRIBES RAIL EMBARKATION

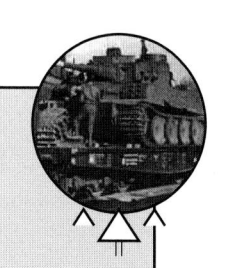

"A PW states that the narrow loading tracks for Tiger tanks belong permanently on the special platform truck and are put back on it when the truck returns to its home station.

Tiger tanks only just fit on the width of the truck and are secured by laying wooden beams against the inner sides of the trucks and securing them to the flooring by means of heavy bolts passing through prepared holes.

One PW described the loading of Tiger tanks at Maille-Le-Camp (France) early in Feb 44 and the unloading a few days later at Ficulie (Italy).

"Conditions at both ends were very bad. Deep mud, rain or snow, and biting winds hindered operations and made the job very trying.

The 80 ton platform truck was shunted up to an end loading ramp and secured in position.

By means of an 18 ton half tracked towing vehicle, the narrow loading tracks were towed off the platform truck and manoeuvred into position on the ground in echelon and at the correct width apart. One broad track was then undone and the tank driven forward on one track so that the bogie wheels on the opposite side ran off the broad track onto the narrow track.

The intended joining point of the narrow track was between the driving sprocket and the ground. To bring the upper run of the track round the rear idler and over the tops of the bogie wheels, the sprocket hub was used as a capstan by passing a wire rope round it. With the broad track locked and the sprocket on the opposite side rotating slowly, the crew pulled on the end of the wire rope and so brought the track up and over.

Having joined the first narrow track, the broad track on the opposite side was undone and the tank driven forward on the narrow track until the bogie wheels ran over the second narrow track.

Once the tank was fitted with the narrow tracks, the crew had to remove the four outside bogie wheels on both sides.

When this had been done, the half tracked towing vehicle had to tow the broad tracks side by side in front of the loading ramp.

The Tiger was then driven forward so that it straddled the tracks on the ground. Wire ropes were attached to the two lifting eyes at the front of the turret, passed over the front armour and secured at their other ends to the tracks.

The Tiger was finally driven up the ramp, towing its own broad tracks underneath it between the narrow tracks. Once it was in position on the platform truck the ultimate operation was to bring up the overhanging ends of the broad tracks over the rear armour of the tank, a feat accomplished by wire ropes and pulleys, with the attendant towing vehicle providing the motive power.

Before the tank was ready to travel, the turret had to be traversed to approx 5 o'clock to allow for the right-handed tunnels which are mostly encountered on the route from France to Italy."

The cumbersome process of preparing the Tiger I for rail transport included removing the outermost road wheels, changing the wide combat tracks to fit the narrow guage tracks shown here.

THE CONTEMPORARY VIEW NO. 8
GERMAN HEAVY TANK
– Pz. Kw. 6

> The accompanying sketch of the tank is based on photographs of a Pz. Kw. 6 knocked out on the Tunisian front.
>
> **SUSPENSION SYSTEM OF PzKw 6**
>
> The suspension system, which has only very briefly been described in Tactical and Technical Trends, is shown in the sketch The track is made of metal. To the far right in the sketch is the front-drive sprocket and to the far left, the rear Idler. There are no return rollers since the track rides on top of the Christie-type wheels, which are rubber rimmed. It will be noted that there are eight axles, each with three wheels to a side, or each with one single and one double wheel to a side. There are thus 24 wheels, or 8 single wheels and 8 double wheels, on each side of the tank. The system of overlapping is similar to the suspension system used on German half-tracks.
>
> The tank is provided with two tracks, a wide one (2 ft, 4.5 in) and a narrow one (just under 2 ft). The wide track is the one used in battle, the narrow being for administrative marches and where manoeuvrability and economy of operation take precedence over ground pressure. The dotted line in the sketch of the suspension system indicates the outer edge of the narrow track. When the narrow track is used, the eight wheels outside the dotted line can be removed.

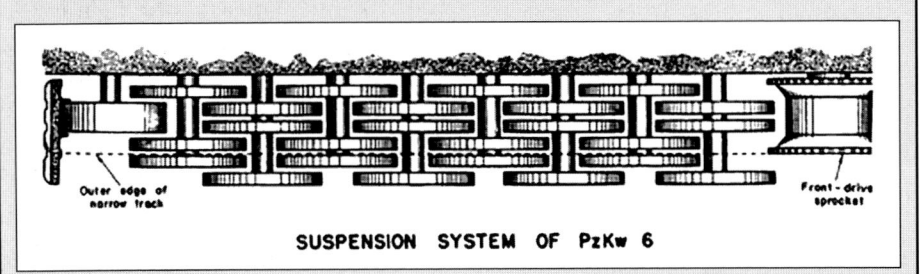

THE CONTEMPORARY VIEW NO.9
USE OF Pz. Kw. VI (TIGER)

"(a) Information obtained from PW indicates that the Pz. Kw. VI was chiefly used in Tunisia to support other armoured units, and mention was made of its employment as mobile artillery. As a support tank it was always used in rear of lighter units. In one reported skirmish however, the lighter Pz. Kw. IIIs and IVs formed the spearhead of the advance; as soon as our tanks came within range the German 'spearhead' tanks deployed to the flanks, leaving the heavier Pz. Kw. VI tanks to engage.

(b) A PW who was with RHQ7 Pz. Regiment in Tunisia for sometime states that there were some 20 Pz. Lw. Vis in the regiment. When on the march ten of these moved with the main column, the others moving on the flanks. According to this PW, the tactics in the attack were to seek to engage enemy tanks from hull-down positions at short ranges, even down to 250 yards. On the other hand, this prisoner also reports an engagement in which two Pz. Kw. Vis brought indirect fire to bear, observation being carried out by an artillery FOO, each tank opening with one round of smoke. In confirmation of this there is another A.F.HQ. report which speaks of this exploitation by Pz. Kw. VI gunners of the great range of their 8.8 cm guns.

(c) 30 Military Mission also reports the use of Pz. Kw. VI in squadron strength on various parts of the Russian Front, especially the South-West.

(d) In conversation with Gerneral Martel, Marshal Stalin stated that in Russia, as in the desert, the Pz. Kw. VI went into battle in rear of a protective screen of lighter tanks.

(e) An A.F.HQ. training instruction states that the size and weight of the Pz. Kw. VI present many problems. PW indicated that extensive reconnaissance of terrain, bridges etc., was necessary before operations with this tank could be undertaken. Bridges had to be reinforced in many cases, and it was necessary for the 'going' to be good for the effective employment of the Pz. Kw. VI."

THE CONTEMPORARY VIEW NO. 10
TIGERS BOLDLY USED

This is a standard Tiger tank - or, as the Germans designate it, Pz. Kpfw. Tiger. (The Roman numeral "VI" has been dropped.)

"At first his Tigers were very boldly used and, once they were sure that their flanks were secured, they drove straight on. After several of these tanks had been knocked out, however, the crews appeared to be less enterprising and were inclined to use their tanks as mobile pillboxes. The fact remains, however, that in an armoured attack the Tiger tank must be regarded as a very formidable fighting component and, given adequate flank protection, will add very effective weight to the enemy firepower.

In the defensive the Pz. Kw. VI, usually well sited in a covered and defiladed position, was a particular danger. Despite the comparatively slow traversing rate of its turret, the Pz. Kw. VI proved an extremely good defensive weapon and could effectively cover a wide area with anti-tank fire. It was often used in good hull-down positions over very difficult ground, which made it hard for the Sherman to deal with it, and no amount of artillery fire could force it out.

Pz. Kw. VIIIs and IVs rarely took up good defensive positions on their own, but were used to watch the flanks of positions occupied by Pz. Kw. VIs. They were often used in small groups to counter-attack from concealed positions on the flank, from a cactus or olive grove or down a wadi. The terrain forced the enemy to employ rush tactics in close formation, and resulted in these counter-attacks being suitably dealt with.

Tank recovery requires a special note. It was often affected on the spot with speed and courage by attaching tow ropes to the casualties and towing them away by other tanks. Special trips at night were made by tanks to recover casualties (20 Jan BOU ARADA, and 1 Feb ROBAA). Where the enemy held the battlefield, tractors were brought up and the whole area cleared of recoverable casualties, both theirs and ours, in a very short time. The speed with which the recovery plan was made and carried out made action by our demolition squads very difficult, and where tank casualties were in no-man's land and unapproachable by day, the enemy would get out to them the moment darkness fell. Sometimes (eg ROBAA, BOU ARADA) as much as a company of infantry was used to hold off our patrols or stage a diversion while recovery was in progress. The enemy used tanks against our Churchills and was quick to take advantage of an unprotected flank

A broken down Tiger I being towed by two Sd.Kfz. 9. The convolutd arrangement was the only means by which a broken donw Tiger I could be officially recovered.

THE CONTEMPORARY VIEW NO. II
GEAR BOX TROUBLE

"If a Tiger tank has gearbox trouble, it is customary to dismantle the flexible couplings in the half-shaft drives and to tow it out of the immediate battle area by another Tiger, using two tow ropes secured in 'X' formation to correct the tendency of the towed tank to sway.

Should, however, the track on a Tiger have ridden up over the sprocket teeth, the tractive effort required to move it is so great that two Tigers pull in tandem, each towing with crossed tow ropes."

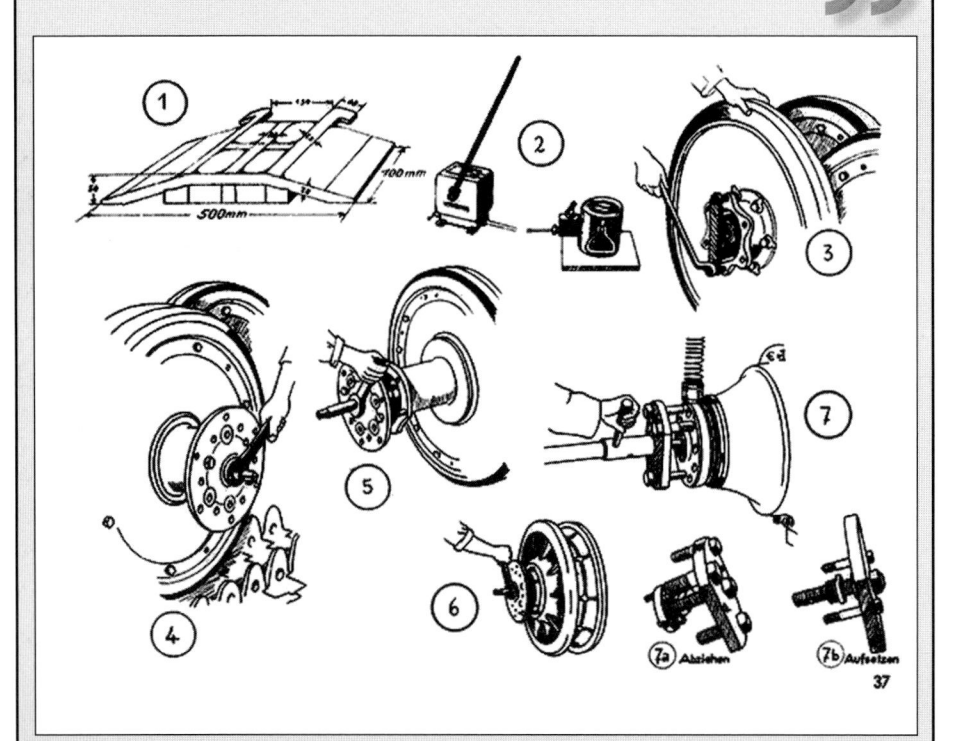

Illustration showing the tools and methods of running gear maintenance from Tigerfibel. Although the need to change road wheels was a frequent and frustrating occurrance, by far the largest share of the mechanical problems resulted from the gear box, the repair of which necessitated the removal of the turret by a mobile crane.

MOBILITY

Despite its drawbacks the Tiger was relatively manoeuvrable for its weight and size, and as it generated less ground pressure, it proved to be superior to the Sherman in muddy terrain,. The Tiger tank however was plainly too heavy to cross small bridges with certainty, so it was purpose designed with the built in mechanism to enable the tank to ford four-meter deep water while fully submerged. This required unusual mechanisms for ventilation and cooling when underwater. At least 30 minutes of set-up was required, with the turret and gun being locked in the forward position, and a large snorkel tube raised at the rear. Only the first 495 Tigers were fitted with this expensive and rarely used deep fording system; all later models were capable of fording only two meters.

The main source of mechanical breakdown of the Tiger I appears to have been the gearbox which is a recurring theme in relation to the numerous breakdowns suffered by these vehicles. Towing a Tiger was an enormous problem and frequently resulted in the breakdown of other Tigers assigned to tow broken down vehicle. The procedure was described in an R.A.C. liaison letter dated August 1944.

The real Achilles heel of the Tiger was the extent to which it was prone to mechanical breakdowns. Even when the vehicle was running smoothly vigilance and extreme care was required as the Tiger was exceptionally liable to becoming bogged down while moving across the difficult terrain which was particularly prevalent in Italy. It was here that the British discovered an inordinately large number of disabled Tigers. Initially these 12 machines were all thought to be victims of combat, but it was later discovered, through examination and prisoner interrogation, that the casualties were all as a result of either mechanical or terrain difficulties. This astonishing revelation was published in August 1944 in a report by the British Army's Technical Branch entitled *"Who Killed Tiger?"*

THE CONTEMPORARY VIEW NO.12
WHO KILLED TIGER?

This Tiger of the 502nd overturned in the act of crossing a bridge in Russia, during November 1943. The tank commander was killed but the tank was recovered.

"As a fairly large number of Tiger tanks were reported to have been knocked out in the breakout from the Anzio bridgehead and the advance on Rome we thought it might be educational to try and find out what weapon or what tactics had been responsible, so that the dose might be repeated on other occasions.

Hearing that there was somewhat of a concentration of bodies in a certain area we made a reconnaissance on the 5th August in an area between Velletri and Cori some 30 miles S.E. of Rome.

In all during this reconnaissance 12 Tigers were found either on the road, by the roadside or within easy sight of the road. The following is what we found:

(1) On the Via Tuscolana. Pulled up at the side of the road near a bridge

diversion. No sign of battle damage but both tracks were off and each had been cut with a gas torch. Blown up and burnt out so the cause of the casualty could not be determined.

(2) On the village green of Giulianello. No sign of battle damage other than a penetration of the hull back plate by Bazooka. This is thought to have been done by following troops after the tank had been abandoned, because the engine cooling fan had been penetrated by the shot but was obviously not rotating at the time and, furthermore, several unused rounds of U.S. Bazooka ammunition were found lying near the machine. This tank had not been demolished by the crew and there was no indication of the cause of stoppage.

(3) By the side of the road one mile from Giulianello. Signs of two H.E. strikes on the turret and one on the cupola. A further H.E. had struck the upper side plate about track level and may have broken the track which was off on this side.

On the opposite side the three rear bogie spindles were bent upwards and the bogies were riding the track guides. A tow-rope was found in place and the tank had been demolished. If the right hand track had in fact been cut by H.E. it is possible that a recovery crew had been caught while extricating the tank which had become a casualty due to the suspension trouble on the other side.

A Tiger I undergoing engine repair.

The task of extricating a stricken Tiger from difficult terrain was beyond every vehicle except another Tiger. Activities of this nature placed a huge strain on the engine and could often result in both vehicles being lost and was officially against orders. However this type of activity, although frowned upon, was a daily occurrence for the men of the Panzerwaffe as there was simply no alternative.

(4) Halfway down a steep bank on the Guilianello-Cori road. No sign of any battle damage or suspension trouble. Tank had been demolished. In this case it is possible that the machine had either become ditched down the bank or had some internal mechanical trouble which could not be rectified.

An interesting point is that this tank had rubber bogie wheels on one side and steel on the other.

(5) Found in a small copse about 100 yards off the road. No sign of battle damage but tank appeared to have become ditched in a sunken lane where it had been trying to turn. Broken tow-ropes found in place. No important suspension defects so that the casualty must have been due to internal mechanical trouble possibly caused by trying to extricate itself from the lane. Blown up.

(6) Found off the road down a bank where it had been pushed to clear the road. Deep A.P. scoops on front of manlet and side of turret. Penetration by unknown weapon through 3rd bogie from rear on left hand side.

Tracks off, blown up and burnt out. Not enough evidence to deduce the cause of the casualty except that it was certainly not due to the A.P. strikes which were probably sustained in an earlier engagement.

(7) Off the road at the edge of an olive grove. Definite evidence of track trouble. Several track guide lugs broken. R.H. sprocket ring cracked in one place and L.H. ring in two places. Attempts to tow had been made. Demolished. Possibly on tow because of mechanical trouble and abandoned when tracks rode the sprockets and damaged them.

(8) On the level in an olive grove. There were signs of the area having been used by a workshop detachment. No apparent battle damage other than penetrations of bogie wheels by H.E. splinters. Casualty probably due to internal mechanical trouble. One demolition charge had been blown.

(9) Found up against a house in Cori where it would appear to have been left by a recovery team. Two H.E. scoops on front plate. Tracks off and obvious signs of suspension trouble. R.H. front bogie bent and out of line. Tracks found near. These showed fractures of several links. Demolished.

Two Tigers of the 504th Schwere Abteilung irrecoverably stuck in a steep valley. This battalion suffered six total write-offs in four days while on a road march in Italy in September 1944.

(10) Off the road in Cori within 10 yards of No.9 above. One bogie wheel missing and others damaged. Sprockets cracked in three places. Tracks off and lying nearby showed evidence of trouble – cracked link and broken guide lug. Demolished.

(11) On the bridge at Cori. Within 50 yards of Nos 9/10. Tank had fallen through damaged arch of bridge. Both tracks off and laid out on the road behind. No battle damage to be seen. Demolished. The presence of Nos 9,10 and 11 tanks so close together suggests that Cori may have been a recovery point for tanks with mechanical trouble which were blown up when it was found impossible to repair them.

(12) Found on the road from Giulianello to Valmontone in a field by a stream some 300 yards off the road. No battle damage but two bogie wheels on one side were bent and out of line. Tracks were still on. There was evidence in the shrubs nearby that the crew of a recovery section had camped by the tank and had been attempting some mechanical repairs which could not be completed in time so that the tank had to be left and demolished.

NOTES

Since the above examination was made some information has been received from a P.O.W. which suggests that these 12 tanks were the remnant of 3 Sqn, 506 Heavy Tank Battalion, which was given the job of resisting the Allied break-out from Anzio with 16 tanks.

Some were lost in the engagement while others suffered gearbox trouble and had to be towed out of action. The squadron was ordered to retreat on Cori and during this retreat so much trouble was experienced with the gearboxes and suspensions of towing tanks that attempts at extrication beyond Cori had to be abandoned.

CONCLUSION

Tiger is not yet sufficiently developed to be considered a reliable vehicle for long marches. He suffers from frequent suspension defects and probably also gearbox trouble. When pushed, as in a retreat, these troubles are too frequent and serious for the German maintenance and recovery organization to deal with.

TIGER RECOVERY

Due to its size and weight the high number of breakdowns and the recovery of battle damaged vehicles was to prove a real headache for the engineers. The tanks were immensely valuable and had to be recovered if at all possible. However, the infrastructure and, in particular the recovery vehicles, to support the easy recovery of such a heavy machine as the Tiger I was found to be severely wanting.

Three famo 18t tractors were needed to drag this Tiger I into the workshop during the assault on Kharkov in 1943.

The main problem was that the standard German heavy Famo recovery half-track tractor could not actually tow the tank; up to three Famo tractors were usually the only way to tow just one Tiger. It was the case therefore that another Tiger was needed to tow a disabled machine, but on such occasions, the engine of the towing vehicle often overheated and sometimes resulted in an engine breakdown or fire. Tiger tanks were therefore forbidden by regulations to tow crippled comrades.

In practice this order was routinely disobeyed as the alternative was the total loss of a large number of tanks that could otherwise have been saved. It was also discovered too late that the low-mounted sprocket limited the obstacle-clearing height. The wide Tiger tracks also had a bad tendency to override the sprocket, resulting in immobilisation. If a track overrode and jammed, two Tigers were normally needed to tow the tank. The jammed track was also a big problem itself, since due to high tension, it was often impossible to disassemble the track by removing the track pins. It was sometimes simply blown apart with an explosive charge.

The illustration from the driver section from Tigerfibel.

THE CONTEMPORARY VIEW NO.13
USE OF Pz. Kw. VI (TIGER)

A section of Tiger I tanks rolls into position prior to the battle of Kursk.

(a) Information obtained from POW indicates that the Pz. Kw. VI was chiefly used in Tunisia to support other armoured units, and mention was made of its employment as mobile artillery. As a support tank it was always used in rear of lighter units. In one reported skirmish however, the lighter Pz. Kw. IIIs and IVs formed the spearhead of the advance; as soon as our tanks came within range the German 'spearhead' tanks deployed to the flanks, leaving the heavier Pz. Kw. VI tanks to engage.

(b) A POW who was with RHQ7 Pz. Regiment in Tunisia for sometime states that there were some 20 Pz. Lw. Vis in the regiment. When on the march ten of these moved with the main column, the others moving on the flanks. According to this PW, the tactics in the attack were to seek to engage enemy tanks from hull-down positions at short ranges, even down to 250 yards. On the other hand, this prisoner also reports an engagement in which two Pz. Kw. VIs brought indirect fire to bear, observation being carried out by an artillery FOO, each tank opening with one round of smoke. In confirmation

A rare shot of a Tiger actually engaged in combat during the battle of Kursk.

of this there is another A.F.HQ. report which speaks of this exploitation by Pz. Kw. VI gunners of the great range of their 8.8 cm guns.

(c) 30 Military Mission also reports the use of Pz. Kw. VI in squadron strength on various parts of the Russian Front, especially the South-West.

(d) In conversation with General Martel, Marshal Stalin stated that in Russia, as in the desert, the Pz. Kw. VI went into battle in rear of a protective screen of lighter tanks.

(e) An A.F.HQ. training instruction states that the size and weight of the Pz. Kw. VI present many problems. PW indicated that extensive reconnaissance of terrain, bridges etc., was necessary before operations with this tank could be undertaken. Bridges had to be reinforced in many cases, and it was necessary for the 'going' to be good for the effective employment of the Pz. Kw. VI.

(f) It would seem that the employment of this tank in a support role is not however invariable, because a German press report of the fighting round Kharkov in March seems to indicate that the Pz. Kw. VI were used offensively in an independent role.

(g) Another German press report states that during the German withdrawal from Schusselburg, 'a few' Pz. Kw. VI formed the most rearward element of the German rearguard, a role in which they were most successful.

(h) An interesting and detailed newspaper article, written towards the end of May, on events on the Leningrad Front, points towards the use of the Tiger as a mobile defensive front and as having been in action 'for days' (i.e. by inference, that they had been in the same area). These operations were carried out in close co-operation with the infantry manning the defensive positions.

In one particular operation a troop of tanks is described as taking up a defensive position forward of the infantry positions from which (presumably hull-down) advancing Soviet tanks and the following infantry were engaged. All this defensive fire was put down at the halt including the fire from the MGs in the tanks. In order to move to an alternative position because of enemy arty fire it was necessary for the tank commander to obtain permission from the CO Battle Group, under whose command he was operating.

CONCLUSION

The use of Pz. Kw. VI tanks in both attack and defence seems, from all available information to hand, to be in a support role. The use of this type of tank in an independent thrusting role, even when supported by tanks of lighter types, would seem to be discouraged.

Distant Tigers moving up to engage Russian forces during the Kursk offensive. The millions of anti-tank mines were the greatest danger facing the Tigers during the assault phase of the battle.

TIGER COLOUR SCHEMES

In June of 1940 a general order was issued that stipulated all Panzers were to be painted *Dunkelgrau* (dark grey). This order was still in effect when the Tigers were initially deployed in August 1942. The very first Tiger I's were painted dark grey and as such are usually easy to identify in photographs.

In areas where winter camouflage was needed, the crews applied whitewash. When spring arrived, the crews had to scrub the whitewash off, which was a tedious, labour intensive chore.

In February 1943, a general order came down to change the base coat from dark grey to tan (Dunkelgelb nach Muster). Crews were issued cans of red brown (Rotbraun) and dark olive green (Olivgruen) to use in creating camouflage patterns over the basic tan colouration.

Some tigers were coated with the Zimmerit anti-magnetic mine coating starting in July 1943. This paste was applied in recognizable grooved patterns and the paint was applied over the top of the coating. Vehicles coated with Zimmerit have a distinctive rough look to their surface.

Camouflage patterns varied from unit to unit, as did the placement and colouring of the vehicle numbers. In addition to good camouflage the tanks themselves required close protection from infantry squads at all times.

A Tiger I painted in the original factory Dunkelgrau deployed on the Northern sector in January 1943.

THE CONTEMPORARY VIEW NO.14
USE OF A F Vs IN NORTH AFRICA

"(a) A POW has described how riflemen with MGs were employed for the protection of tanks when in harbour. On the following morning they were withdrawn from this task for rest and in preparation for other duties.

(b) A POW reports that German tanks were always able to intercept Allied radio traffic, on one occasion obtaining in this way an exact location. Pz. Kw. VI were immediately detailed to engage.

(c) Voluntary destruction of tanks. On 5th December 1942 the following orders were issued by OC 8 Pz. Regiment: "Tanks may be blown up in the following circumstances only:

(i) If the tank cannot be moved

(ii) If the enemy is attacking, and then only,

(iii) If the tank has defended itself to its last round.

The Commander responsible for issuing the order to blow up the tank must make a report to R H Q detailing the circumstances".

(d) Another report describes as 'typical' a case in which a large concentration of tanks was observed opposite one area on our front, small parties of which were observed 'tapping' along our front, halting to fire from about 2,000 yards.

(e) On another occasion another report describes how an estimated total of 50 German tanks put in a counter-attack in the early evening in two groups, each under smoke cover."

The radio operator from the Tigerfibel.

DESIGN REVIEW

As the war wore on into 1944 the increasing volume of captured Tigers continued to yield invaluable intelligence information. With a number of complete machines now in the hands of the western allies it was possible to conduct increasingly scientific examinations. Practical testing of weapon systems and armour was soon undertaken to identify the strengths and weaknesses of the Tiger I. In November 1944 a series of gunnery trials was conducted by Major W. de L. Messenger and his report is summarized overleaf.

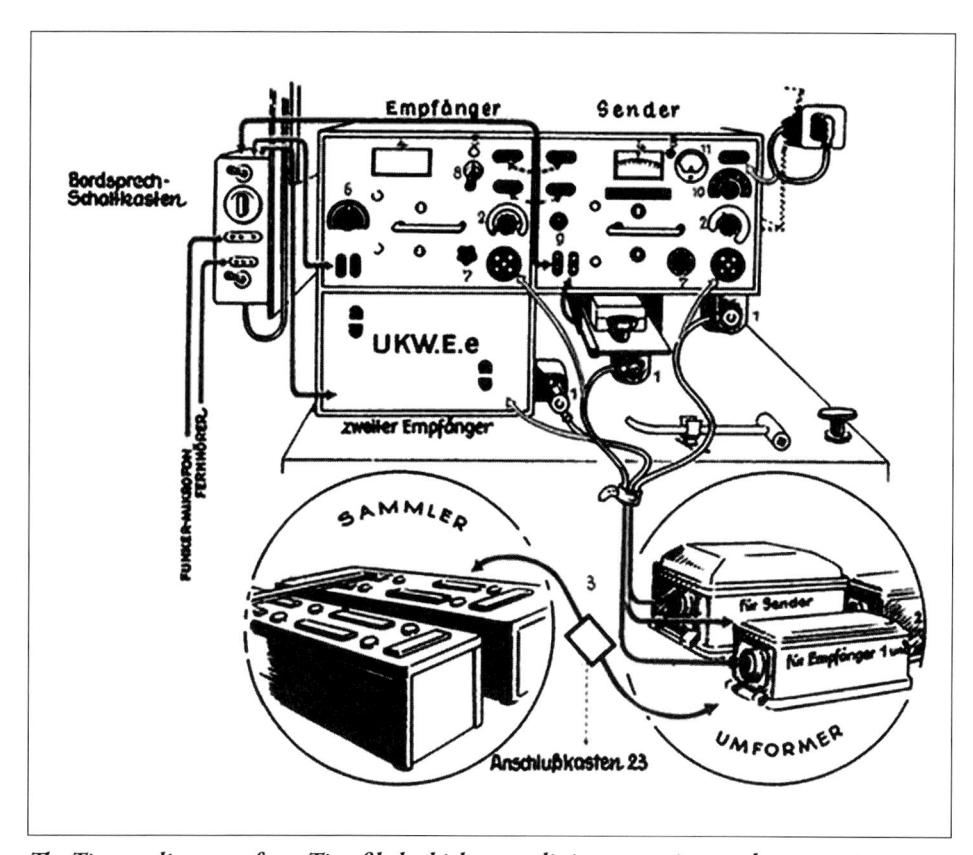

The Tiger radio set up from Tigerfibel which was split into a receiver and a transmitter.

THE CONTEMPORARY VIEW NO.15
DESIGN REVIEW

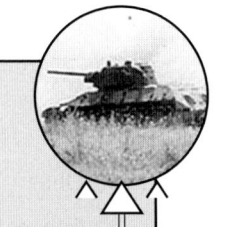

"The design has been well thought out and it embodies a number of distinctly original features such as the heavy armament and armour, turret and hull construction, powered traverse layout and facilities for total submersion.

It appears that the user has not had the same influence on it as on British tanks since so many of the items, whilst basically good, are unsatisfactory and could well be improved from the user aspect by slight modification.

The outstanding features would appear to be:

GOOD POINTS

(1) 8.8cm gun with its smooth action and easily stripped breech mechanism.

(2) Heavy armour and method of construction (welding and front plates projecting above the roof plates).

(3) Stability as a gun platform.

(4) Ammunition stowage – quantity and accessibility.

(5) Electrical firing gear with safety interlocks and novel trigger switch.

(6) Flush turret floor without coaming or shields.

(7) Binocular telescope with fixed eyepiece.

(8) Mounting for periscopic binoculars in cupola and commander's hand traverse.

(9) Ability to superimpose hand on power traverse and absence of oil pipes and unions.

(10) Ample space for loader.

(11) Method of attaching stowage to turret walls (flexible strips).

(12) Spring assisted hatches.

(13) S-mine dischargers.

(14) 2-position commander's seat and backrest

(15) Electrically fired smoke generator dischargers.

(16) Handholds on roof to assist gunner.

BAD POINTS

(1) Out-of-balance of gun and turret.

(2) Obscuration by smoke from flashless propellent.

(3) Ventilation of gun fumes

(4) Lack of intercommunication for loader.

(5) Cramped positions of gunner and commander.

(6) Powered traverse control – Lack of definite neutral position and awkward range of movement

(7) No armouring on bins.

(8) Small gun deflector bag.

(9) Awkward re-arming of co-axial M.G.

(10) Gunner's exit via commander's cupola.

(11) Head pad on auxiliary M.G.

The Pz. Kpfw. VI with its heavy armour, dual purpose armament and fighting ability is basically an excellent tank, and, in spite of the defects noted, constitutes a considerable advance on any tank that we have tried.

Its greatest weakness is probably the limit imposed on mobility owing to its weight, width and limited range of action. Taking it all round, it presents a very formidable fighting machine which should not be under-rated."

The Tiger was a prized target and was as vulnerable as any other tank to strongly motivated tank hunting teams. Close support from well trained infantry was therefore crucial to the survival of the Tigers on the battlefield. The Tiger on the right is carrying its own close support team.

PRODUCTION RUN MODIFICATIONS

During the production run of the Tiger I a number of modifications were introduced in order to correct imperfections to improve automotive performance, firepower and protection. Any good measure which led to the simplification of the design was also implemented, along with forced adjustments as a result of shortages of war materials. Due to a rigid production flow policy at the Henschel factory, incorporation of the new modifications could take several months. In 1942 alone, at least six revisions were made, starting with the removal of the *Vorpanzer* (frontal armour shield) from the pre-production models in April 1942. In May, mudguards bolted onto the side of the pre-production run were added, while removable mudguards saw full incorporation in September. Smoke discharge canisters, three on each side of the turret, were added in August 1942. In later years, similar changes and updates were added, such as the addition of Zimmerit in late 1943.

Modifications continued as a result of combat experiences in Italy at a comparatively late stage in the life of the Tiger I. The RAC liaison letter for August 1944 revealed that POW integration sources were still providing valuable information regarding the on-going modification programme, which mentioned modifications in the Model E over its predecessors including the following:-

THE CONTEMPORARY VIEW NO. 16
TURRET TOP ARMOUR

"In early March '44 on the beachhead, a number of Tiger tanks were spotted from the air by an artillery recce aircraft and shortly afterwards a concentration of artillery fire was put down, during which the turret top of one Tiger was pieced by a direct hit from what appears to be an American "Long Tom."

This incident, which cost two dead of the crew, was duly reported and is considered to have been the reason for the thickening of the turret top armour back and front from 25mm to 40mm on the Model E Tigers which came down from Paderborn in late May 1944."

COMBAT HISTORY

As we have see the Tiger was first used in action on 28th September 1942 in marshy terrain near Leningrad. The action was a direct result of Hitler's desperation to see the Tiger in action. This resulted in the tank, which was still very much a prototype, being forced into action prematurely.

Unfortunately, on 22nd September 1942, as they entered the combat arena for the first time the Tigers were deployed single file over marshy terrain with the inevitable result that the machines began to bog down. It was to prove an ominous portent when, in their first day of combat, all four were knocked out. It is interesting to note however that the armour of the vehicles was not penetrated. Three of the Tigers which had been abandoned by their crews were later recovered.

In spite of this atrocious start the Tiger I was to become a fixture of a number of heavy units serving on the eastern front. Better tactics involving close co-operation with supporting infantry units were soon developed and other Panzer crews were quickly trained at Paderborn so that they too could be equipped with the Tiger I as the machines rolled off the production lines. The deployment of

An interesting study of two Tigers passing on a narrow forest track in northern Russia during the summer of 1943.

A Grenadier standing in front of a trio of captured Russian anti-tank guns scans the skies as a Tiger I in summer camouflage paint scheme rolls on towards the enemy.

The Tiger I happened at a fairly rapid pace and by the end of 1942 the first Tiger formations had been deployed in Russia, Tunisia, and Italy. A further training centre was soon established in France. Tigers would eventually be in service with ten Heer heavy tank battalions and one training battalion as well as and the Grossdeutschland Panzer Grenadier Division.

In addition to the regular army units three Waffen-SS heavy tank battalions were also equipped with the Tiger I. A number of additional Heer formations received a smattering of Tigers though the numbers were generally very limited. The 14 Tiger equipped units were the backbone of the fighting force and were issued with the bulk of the available machines.

In the North African theatre, the Tiger first saw action near Robaa Tunisia. In the ensuing battle, a battery belonging to the 72nd Anti-tank Regiment of the British Army equipped with six-pounder managed to knock out three enemy Tigers and rout the remaining forces. The action soon found its way into the British and US intelligence reports reprinted elsewhere in this book. The next theatre in which the allies encountered the Tiger was to be Italy where Tigers were encountered both in Sicily and on the mainland. Following the D-Day landings the Tiger I was encountered during the Normandy battles where it was fielded by the Leibstandarte division.

ROAD MARCHES

The Tiger's extreme weight limited which bridges it could cross. It also made driving through buildings something of a lottery as basements were liable to collapse trapping the tank in the rubble. Another weakness was the slow traverse of the hydraulically-operated turret. The turret could also be traversed manually, but this option was laborious and rarely used, except for very small adjustments.

Early Tigers had a top speed of about 45 kilometres per hour (28mph) over optimal terrain. This was not recommended for normal operation, and was discouraged in training. Crews were ordered not to exceed 2600rpm due to reliability problems of the early Maybach engines with their maximum 3000rpm output. To combat this, the Tiger's top speed was reduced to about 38 kilometres per hour (24mph) through the installation of an engine governor, capping the rpm of the Maybach HL 230 to 2600rpm (HL 210s were used on early models). Despite being slower than medium tanks of the time, which averaged a top speed of about 45 kilometres per hour (28mph), the Tiger still had a very respectable

Another shot of a Tiger I encountering difficult terrain and insurmountable obstacles in the Army Group North sector.

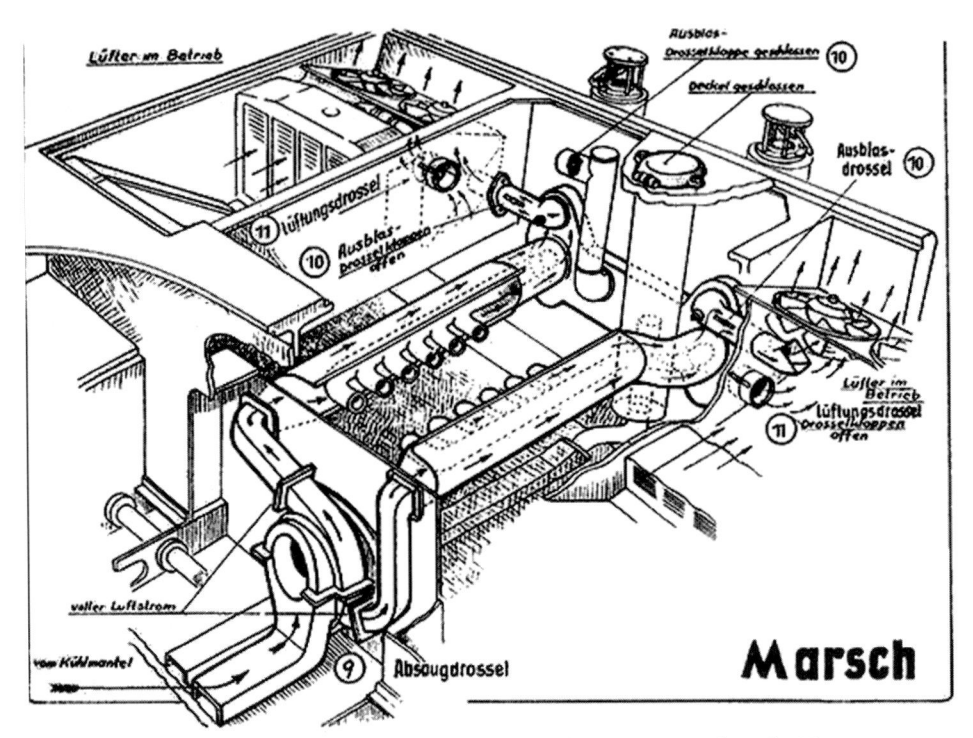

This diagram from Tigerfibel shows throttle and vent flap positions when the Tiger is moving on a road march.

speed for a tank of its size and weight, especially if one considers the fact that the Tiger I was nearly twice as heavy as a Sherman or T-34.

The Tiger had reliability problems throughout its service life; Tiger units almost invariably entered combat under strength due to various mechanical breakdowns. It was rare for any Tiger unit to complete a road march without losing vehicles due to breakdowns. The tank also had poor radius of action ie the distance which a combat vehicle can travel and return to the battlefield without refuelling. Although the Tigerfibel gave the figure of 42.5km in each direction (see page 27) the reality was much lower - 35km across country was considered to be the maximum on a full tank. However, the Tiger I was a remarkably efficient cross-country vehicle. Due to its very wide tracks however, the Tiger did produce a lower ground pressure bearing than many smaller tanks, the most notable exception being the Soviet T-34 which also ran on comparatively wide tracks.

THE CONTEMPORARY VIEW NO.17
NOTES ON TANK TACTICS USE OF PZ KW VI (TIGER)

"Information obtained from PW indicates that the Pz Kw VI was chiefly used in Tunisia to support other armoured units, and mention was made of its employment as mobile artillery. As a support tank it was always used in rear of

lighter units. In one reported skirmish however, the lighter Pz Kw IIIs and IVs formed the spearhead of the advance; as soon as our tanks came within range the German 'spearhead' tanks deployed to the flanks, leaving the heavier Pz Kw VI tanks to engage.

A PW who was with RHQ7 Pz Regiment in Tunisia for some time states that there were some 20 Pz Kw Vis in the regiment. When on the march ten of these moved with the main column, the others moving on the flanks. According to this PW, the tactics in the attack were to seek to engage enemy tanks from hull-down positions at short ranges, even down to 250 yards. On the other hand, this prisoner also reports an engagement in which two Pz Kw Vis brought indirect fire to bear, observation being carried out by an artillery F O O, each tank opening with one round of smoke. In confirmation of this there is another A.F.HQ report which speaks of this exploitation by Pz Kw VI gunners of the great range of their 8.8 cm guns.

30 Military Mission also reports the use of Pz Kw VI in squadron strength on various parts of the Russian Front, especially the South-West.

In conversation with General Martel, Marshal Stalin stated that in Russia, as in the desert, the Pz Kw VI went into battle in rear of a protective screen of lighter tanks.

An A.F.HQ. training instruction states that the size and weight of the Pz Kw VI present many problems. PW indicated that extensive reconnaissance of terrain, bridges etc., was necessary before operations with this tank could be undertaken. Bridges had to be reinforced in many cases, and it was necessary for the 'going' to be good for the effective employment of the Pz Kw VI.

It would seem that the employment of this tank in a support role is not however invariable, because a German press report of the fighting round Kharkov in March seems to indicate that the Pz Kw VI were used offensively in an independent role.

Another German press report states that during the German withdrawal from Schusselburg, a "few" Pz Kw VI formed the most rearward element of the German rearguard, a role in which they were most successful.

An interesting and detailed newspaper article, written towards the end of May, on events on the Leningrad Front, points towards the use of the Tiher as a mobile defensive pillbox. The tanks are described as operation on a defensive front and as having been in action 'for days' (i.e. by inference, that they had been in the same area). These operations were carried out in close co-operation with the infantry manning the defensive positions.

In one particular operation a troop of tanks is described as taking up a defensive position forward of the infantry positions from which (presumably hull-down) advancing Soviet tanks and the following infantry were engaged. All this defensive fire was put down at the halt including the fire from the MGs in the tanks. In order to move to an alternative position because of enemy arty fire it was necessary for the tank commander to obtain permission from the CO Battle Group. under whose command he was operating.

The use of Pz Kw VI tanks in both attack and defence seems, from all available information to hand, to be in a support role. The use of this type of tank in an independent thrusting role, even when supported by tanks of lighter types, would seem to be discouraged.**"**

The loader from Tigerfibel.

TACTICAL ORGANISATION

The Tiger I was usually employed in separate heavy tank battalions known as schwere-Panzer-Abteilung, and were so precious they were generally placed under army command. The heavy battalions would normally be deployed to critical sectors, for use either in breakthrough operations or, as the war wore on, more typically in local counter-attacks. A few favoured divisions, such as the Grossdeutschland and the 1st SS Leibstandarte Adolf Hitler, 2nd SS Das Reich, and 3rd SS Totenkopf Panzergrenadier Divisions at Kursk had a Tiger company in their tank regiments. The Grossdeutschland Division had its Tiger company increased to a battalion as the III Panzer Battalion in Panzer Regiment

The commanders chosen to be granted command of a Tiger I represented the very best of the candidates who passed through the gates of the tank training facility at Paderborn.

Grossdeutschland. 3rd SS Totenkopf retained its Tiger I company through the remainder of the war. 1st SS and 2nd SS tank regiments lost their Tiger Companies which were incorporated into a SS Tiger Battalion, the 101st SS Tiger Battalion, which was part of 1st SS Panzer Korps.

The Tiger was originally designed to be an offensive breakthrough weapon, but by the time they went into action, the military situation had changed dramatically, and their main use was on the defensive, as mobile gun batteries known as "the mobile fire brigade". Unfortunately, this also meant rushing the Tigers constantly from location to location causing excessive mechanical issues. As a result, there are almost no instances where a Tiger battalion went into combat at anything close to full strength. Furthermore, against the Soviet and Western Allied production numbers, even a 10:1 kill ratio would not have been sufficient to turn the tactical tide. Some Tiger units did actually exceed the 10:1 kill ratio, including 13. Kompanie/Panzer-Regiment Grossdeutschland with a ratio of 16:1, schwere SS-Panzer-Abteilung 103 with a ratio of 12:1 and schwere Panzer-Abteilung 502 with a ratio of 13:1. These numbers must be set against the opportunity cost of the expensive Tiger. Every Tiger cost as much as four Sturmgeschütz III assault guns to build.

An English translation of a contemporary article from the Soviet Artillery Journal giving detailed instructions for the use of anti-tank weapons against the German Tiger tank, appeared in the U.S. intelligence periodical *Tactical and Technical Trends*, No. 40, December 16th, 1943. Vulnerability of various parts of the tank was cited in connection with directions for attack. At the time of publication, U.S. forces had only sporadically encountered the Tiger tank in Tunisia, Sicily, and Italy. The accompanying sketch shows vulnerable points and indicates weapons to be used against them. Material concerning the vulnerability of German tanks was published in Tactical and Technical Trends No. 8, p. 46 and No. 11, p.28. Detailed information about the Tiger tank was published in Tactical and Technical Trends No. 34, p.13. A translation of the Soviet Artillery Journal article follows overleaf:

THE RUSSIAN VIEW
VULNERABILITY OF TIGER TANKS

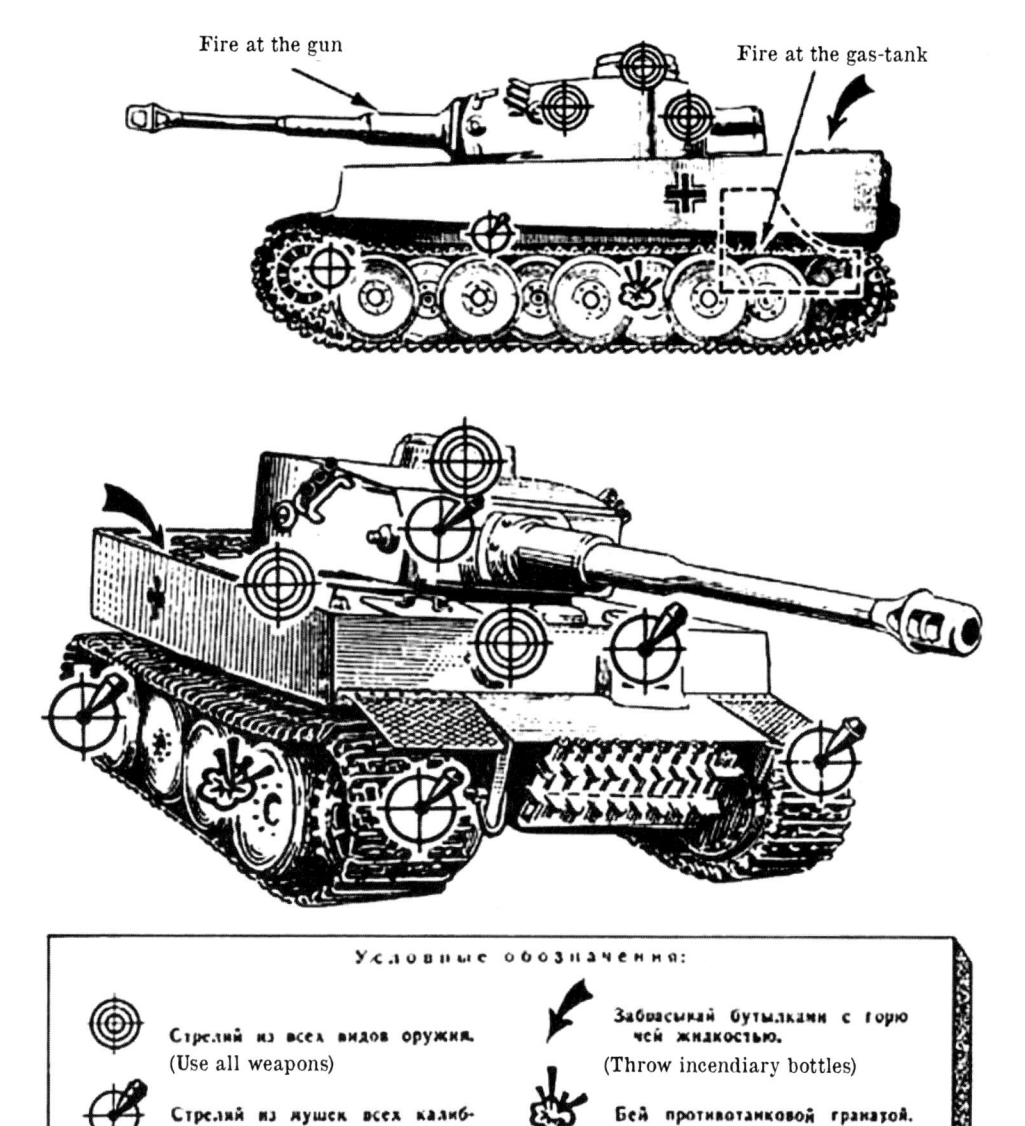

Fire at the gun

Fire at the gas-tank

Условные обозначения:

◎ Стреляй из всех видов оружия.
(Use all weapons)

⊘ Стреляй из пушек всех калибров.
(Use guns of all calibers)

↘ Забрасывай бутылками с горючей жидкостью.
(Throw incendiary bottles)

✊ Бей противотанковой гранатой.
(Use AT grenades)

The Russian view on how to attack the Tiger was reproduced for the benefit of western Allied soldiers in the December 1943 version of Tactical and Technical Trends.

THE CONTEMPORARY VIEW NO.18
VULNERABILITY OF TIGER TANKS

"The mobility of tanks depends upon the proper functioning of the suspension parts - sprocket (small driving wheel), idler (small wheel in the rear), wheels and tracks. All of these parts are vulnerable to shells of all calibres. A particularly vulnerable part is the sprocket.

"Fire armour-piercing shells and HE shells at the sprocket, the idler and the tracks. This will stop the tank. Fire at the wheels with HE shells. Also, when attacking a tank, use AT grenades and mines. If movable mines are used, attach three or four of them to a board and draw the board, by means of a cord or cable, into the path of an advancing tank.

"There are two armour plates on each side of the tank. The lower plate is partly covered by the wheels. This plate protects the engine and the gasoline tanks which are located in the rear of the hull, directly beyond and over the two rear wheels.

"Fire at the lower plates with armour-piercing shells from 76-, 57- and 45mm guns. When the gasoline tanks are hit, the vehicle will be set on fire. Another method of starting a fire within the tank is to pierce the upper plates on the sides of the tank, thus reaching the ammunition compartments and causing an explosion.

"The rear armour plate protects the engine as well as giving additional protection to the gasoline tanks. Shells from AT guns, penetrating this armour, will disable the tank.

"The turret has two vision ports and two openings through which the tank's crew fire their weapons. The commander's small turret has five observation slits. There are two sighting devices on the roof of the front of the tank, one for the driver, the other for the gunner. Also, in the front of the tank there is a port with a sliding cover.

"The turret is a particularly important and vulnerable target. Attack it with HE and armour-piercing shells of all calibres. When it is damaged, use AT grenades and incendiary bottles (Molotov cocktails).

"There is a 10mm slit all around the base of the turret. AT gun and heavy machine-gun fire, effectively directed at this slit, will prevent the turret from revolving and thus seriously impair the tank's field of fire. Furthermore, hits by HE shell at the base of the turret may wreck the roof of the hull and put the tank out of action.

"The tank's air vents and ventilators are under the perforations in the roof of the hull, directly behind the turret. Another air vent is in the front part of the roof, between the two observation ports used by the radio operator and the driver. Use AT grenades and incendiary bottles against these vents.

"Explode antitank mines under the tank to smash the floor and put the tank out of action."

A Tiger I camouflaged in a static defensive position.

TIGER ACES

The Tiger is particularly associated with SS-Hauptsturmführer Michael Wittmann of schwere SS-Panzerabteilung 101. He worked his way up, commanding various vehicles and finally a Tiger I. In the Battle of Villers-Bocage, his platoon destroyed over two dozen Allied vehicles, including several tanks.

Astonishingly given his enduring reputation Wittmann was not the highest scoring tank commander. Over ten Tiger tank commanders claimed over 100 vehicle kills each, including Kurt Knispel with 168, Walter Schroif with 161, Otto Carius with 150+, Johannes Bölter with 139+, and Michael Wittmann with 138.

Name	Tank Kills	Unit
Kurt Knispel	168	s.Pz.Abt. 503
Martin Schroif	161	s.SS-Pz.Abt. 102
Otto Carius	150+	s.Pz.Abt. 502
Hans Bolter	139+	s.Pz.Abt. 502
Michael Wittmann	138	s.SS-Pz.Abt. 101
Paul Egger	113	s.SS-Pz.Abt. 102
Arno Giesen	111	8./SS-Pz.Rgt. 2
Heinz Rondorf	106	s.Pz.Abt. 503
Heinz Gartner	103	s.Pz.Abt. 503
Wilhelm Knauth	101+	s.Pz.Abt. 505
Albert Kerscher	100+	s.Pz.Abt. 502
Balthazar Woll	100+	s.SS-Pz.Abt. 101
Karl Mobius	100+	s.SS-Pz.Abt. 101
Helmut Wendorff	95	s.SS-Pz.Abt. 101
Will Fey	80+	s.SS-Pz.Abt. 102
Eric Litztke	76	s.Pz.Abt. 509
Emil Seibold	69	s.SS-Pz.Abt. 502
Karl Brommann	66	s.SS-Pz.Abt. 503

The cover illustration from Tigerfibel

Kurt Knispel

Martin Schroif

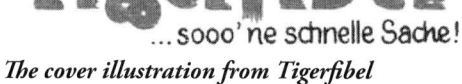

Otto Carius

Hans Bolter

Michael Wittmann

Paul Egger

Heinz Rondorf

Heinz Gartner

Wilhelm Knauth

Albert Kerscher

Bobby Woll

Karl Mobius

Helmut Wendorff    Will Fey    Eric Litztke    Emil Seibold

Karl Brommann    Alfred Rubbel    Konrad Weinert    Walter Junge

Bobby Warmbrunn    Jurgen Brandt    Heinz Kling    Heinz Kramer

Alfredo Carpaneto    Heinz Mausberg    Franz Staudegger

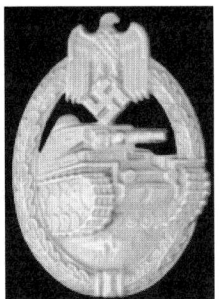

Alfred Rubbel	60+	s.Pz.Abt. 503
Konrad Weinert	59	s.Pz.Abt. 503
Walter Junge	57+	s.Pz.Abt. 503
Bobby Warmbrunn	57	s.SS-Pz.Abt. 101
Jurgen Brandt	57	s.SS-Pz.Abt. 101
Heinz Kling	51+	s.SS-Pz.Abt. 101
Heinz Kramer	50+	s.Pz.Abt. 502
Alfredo Carpaneto	50+	s.Pz.Abt. 502
Heinz Mausberg	50+	s.Pz.Abt. 505
Oskar Geiner	50+	s.SS-Pz.Abt. 103
Johann Muller	50+	s.Pz.Abt. 502
Joachim Scholl	42	s.SS-Pz.Abt. 102
Franz Staudegger	35+	s.SS-Pz.Abt. 101

The Tiger I has been estimated to have an overall ratio of 5.74 kills to each loss, with 9,850 enemy tanks destroyed for a loss of 1,715 Tigers. It is important to note that the number of Tiger Is lost is higher than those produced (1,347), as the Wehrmacht included tanks that had undergone heavy repair and brought back into combat in the total of new machines.

A powerful study of Tigers in action near Orel.

Tiger tank ace Michael Wittmann. Despite all of the reports, it comes as a surprise to many to discover that the highest scoring Tiger I ace was actually Kurt Knispel who survived the war with 168 tank kills to his credit.

The following chart demonstrates the estimated Tiger I kills to losses ratio:

Unit	Losses	Kills	Kill/Loss Ratio
schwere Panzer-Abteilung 501	120	450	3.75
schwere Panzer-Abteilung 502	107	1,400	13.08
schwere Panzer-Abteilung 503	252	1,700	6.75
schwere Panzer-Abteilung 504	109	250	2.29
schwere Panzer-Abteilung 505	126	900	7.14
schwere Panzer-Abteilung 506	179	400	2.23
schwere Panzer-Abteilung 507	104	600	5.77
schwere Panzer-Abteilung 508	78	100	1.28
schwere Panzer-Abteilung 509	120	500	4.17
schwere Panzer-Abteilung 510	65	200	3.08
13./Panzer-Regiment Grossdeutschland	6	100	16.67
III./Panzer-Regiment Grossdeutschland	98	500	5.10
13./SS-Panzerregiment 1	42	400	9.52
8./SS-Panzerregiment 2	31	250	8.06
9./SS-Panzerregiment 3	56	500	8.93
schwere SS-Panzer-Abteilung 101 (501)	107	500	4.67
schwere SS-Panzer-Abteilung 102 (502)	76	600	7.89
schwere SS-Panzer-Abteilung 103 (503)	39	500	12.82
Total	1,715	9,850	5.74

A Tiger I engages in action during the battle of Kursk.

TIGERPHOBIA

The Tigers forged an impressive combat record in Russia during 1943 and 1944. They destroyed tremendous amounts of enemy equipment especially anti-tank guns. Eventually it was held that often the mere sight of a Tiger was enough to cause Russian tank crews to withdraw from the battlefield. The Tiger enjoyed a similar psychological success in North Africa and Italy, creating a powerful negative effect on the morale of both British and US troops. The mere rumour that the troops were up against Tigers was often enough to spread panic.

The debilitating influence of the Tiger on allied morale was so widespread the condition was given its own name and was widely known as *Tigerphobia*. The grip which the Tiger held on the popular imaginations of allied soldiers was so severe that British Field Marshall Montgomery banned all reports of the Tiger which made any reference to its prowess in battle. There were times when even Monty couldn't prevail over the cold facts. In the right hands the Tiger was a ferociously weapon system. The Tiger's greatest moment of fame was one such moment.

This impactful study of a Tiger I on the move creates a strong impression of the power of the Tiger I. Faced with the prospect of engaging with a fast moving and strongly equipped monster such as this it is easy to understand how the Tigerphobia condition grew and spread.

Panzer crewmen inspect the combat damage inflicted by enemy rounds which have just failed to pierce the strong side armour of the Tiger.

Michael Wittmann gained lasting notoriety with his amazing exploits in a single action on 13th June 1944 in Normandy where the famous commander destroyed an entire column of 25 tanks, 14 half-tracks and 14 bren-gun carriers in a few short minutes with one Tiger I handled with deadly efficiency.

This press photo does a great job of conveying the strength of the frontal armour of a Tiger I which, although not efficiently sloped, was strong and robust enough to deal with the direct hit from a large calibre shell, the evidence of which can be seen on the front mantlet to the right of the figure in the helmet.

THE CONTEMPORARY VIEW NO.19
NOTES ON TIGER TANKS IN THE BATTLE FOR FLORENCE

A field conference in the summer of 1943, the half hearted camouflage and relaxed attitude suggest that soviet air cover was not percievd to be a threat by these tank men.

In the battle for Florence, a New Zealand division had its first experience with standard Tiger tanks on a fairly large scale, and noted several useful points about the ways in which the Germans employed these vehicles.

As a rule, the Tigers were well sited and well camouflaged with natural foliage. To delay the New Zealand infantry and to pick off tanks, the Tigers were used in hull-down positions. Another enemy method was to send Tigers by covered routes to previously selected positions. From these positions the Germans would fire a few harassing rounds, withdraw, and move to alternate positions. Tigers also were used to provide close support for German infantry, to lend additional fire power to artillery concentrations, and to engage buildings occupied by the New Zealanders. These troops noted that almost invariably a Tiger would be sited with at least one other tank or a self-propelled gun in support. The supporting tank or gun would remain silent unless its fire was absolutely needed. Sometimes a Tiger would be accompanied by infantrymen - often only 6 to 12 of them - deployed on the flanks as far as 50 yards away from the tank.

The New Zealanders were of the opinion that the Tiger's heavy front and rear armour made it unlikely that the tank would be knocked out by hits on these parts. Simultaneous frontal and flank attacks were considered desirable. The New Zealanders found the Tigers' side armour definitely vulnerable to fire from 17-pounders. Other weak spots, it was reported, were the rear of the tank, just over the engines, and the large exhaust hole, also in the rear and just over the left of centre. Some commanders found high explosives the most effective ammunition against these rear parts.

As a rule, the Tigers were placed in position so skillfully that the New Zealanders found it difficult to employ a sniping anti-tank gun or a towed gun for stalking purposes. Unless very careful reconnaissance was carried out to site the gun to the best advantage, and so as to detect German supporting tanks or self-propelled guns, the effort was likely to be fruitless. For this reason, the New Zealanders concluded that maximum time for reconnaissance, and the maximum amount of information, were essential for a battery commander who was called upon to engage a Tiger. The German tank-and-gun combination seemed to be slow at manoeuvring and firing, and also very susceptible to blinding by U.S. 75mm smoke ammunition. On one occasion, two smoke rounds, followed by armour-piercing projectiles, were enough to force a Tiger to withdraw.

Sometimes the Germans used their Tigers with marked recklessness, the crews taking risks to an extent which indicated their extreme confidence in their vehicles. This rendered the latter vulnerable to New Zealand tank-hunting squads armed with close-range antitank weapons. When Tigers were closed down, and were attacking on their own at some distance from their supporting guns, the tanks' vulnerability to those close-range weapons was increased correspondingly.

Tigers were effectively knocked out, or were forced to withdraw, by concentrations of field artillery. It was clear that German tank crews feared the damaging effect of shell fire against such vital parts as tracks, suspension, bogie wheels, radio aerials, electrical equipment, and so on.

The New Zealanders incorporated medium artillery in several of their artillery concentrations, and decided that medium pieces were suitable when a sufficiently large concentration could be brought to bear. However, owing to a dispersion of rounds, it was considered preferable to include a good concentration of field guns, to "thicken up" the fire. The division in question had no experience in using heavy artillery against Tigers.

It was admittedly difficult to locate stationary, well camouflaged Tigers which had been sited for defensive firing. Worth mentioning, however, is the performance of an artillery observation post, which was notified by Allied tanks that a Tiger was believed to be in a certain area. The observation post began to range. A round falling in the vicinity of the suspected tank blasted away the vehicle's camouflage, and the Tiger promptly retreated.

Several of the New Zealand antitank gunners' experiences in combating Tigers will be of special interest:

(1) A Tiger was observed about 3,000 yards away, engaging three Shermans. When it set one of the Shermans afire, the other two withdrew over a crest. A 17-pounder was brought up to within 2,400 yards of the Tiger, and engaged it from a flank. When the Tiger realized that it was being engaged by a high-velocity gun, it swung around 90 degrees so that its heavy frontal armour was toward the gun. In the ensuing duel, one round hit the turret, another round hit the suspension, and two near-short rounds probably ricocheted into the tank. The tank was not put out of action. The range was too great to expect a kill; hence the New Zealanders' tactics were to make the Tiger expose its flank to the Shermans at a range of almost 500 yards, by swinging around onto the antitank gun. The Tiger did just this, and, when it was engaged by the Shermans, it withdrew. The enemy infantry protection of half a dozen to a dozen men was engaged by machine guns.

(2) At the junction of a main road and a side road, a Tiger was just off the road, engaging forward troops in buildings. Another Tiger, about 50 yards up the side road, was supporting the first. A field-artillery concentration was called for. It appeared to come from one battery only. Although no hits were observed, both Tigers withdrew.

(3) A Tiger on a ridge was engaged by what appeared to be a battery of mediums. After the first few rounds had fallen, the crew bailed out.

(It is not known why.) Shortly afterward, while the tank still was being shelled, a German soldier returned to the tank and drove it off. About 10 minutes later, the remainder of the crew made a dash along the same route their tank had taken.

(4) A tank hidden in the garage of a two-story house ventured out for about 20 yards, fired a few harassing rounds, and returned to its shelter. Many hits on the building were scored by 4.2-inch mortars firing cap-on, but little damage was visible. Each night the tank was withdrawn from the area, even though it was in an excellent concealed position and was protected by infantry. Later the house was examined. Although it had suffered appreciable damage — and there were several dead Germans about there was no evidence that damage had been done to the tank itself.

A tank man inspects the combat damage inflicted by enemy rounds which have failed to pierce the strong side armour of the Tiger tank turret.

INSIDE THE TIGER

The internal layout was typical of German tanks. Forward was an open crew compartment, with the driver and radio-operator seated at the front on either side of the gearbox. Behind them the turret floor was surrounded by panels forming a continuous level surface. This helped the loader to retrieve the ammunition, which was mostly stowed above the tracks. Two men were seated in the turret; the gunner to the left of the gun, and the commander behind him. There was also a folding seat on the right for the loader. The turret had a full circular floor and 157cm headroom.

The crews of the Tiger tank gained a feeling of invincibility and this mood of superiority on behalf of the German tank crews survived defeat and captivity as revealed by the interrogation of an veteran German tank gunner who had served in The Afrika Korps and in Italy and therefore could boast practical experience of both the Tiger and captured allied Sherman tanks.

This photograph from a contemporary British report shows the driving position of the Tiger I.

THE CONTEMPORARY VIEW NO.20
THE TIGER vs THE SHERMAN

"The gun layer- an experienced tank man- was inclined to be very boastful where German tanks were concerned. He had landed in Africa in May 1941 and stayed in the desert for nearly two years (no home leave and only the rarest visits to towns). His memories of the campaign are chiefly a record of the numbers of British AFVs knocked out by the invincible Mk IIIs and IVs, tinged with a reluctant admission that the same tanks were matched in October 43 at Alamein by General Grants and General Shermans. He was critical of the fact that the employment of these AFVs had not been appreciated by the Germans and that the launching of the British push came as a surprise to the armoured Divs.

His confidence has been fully restored since he transferred to Tiger Tanks. On every occasion he stresses the great feeling of security which a crew has inside an AFV with such armour. Crews feel very certain of their ability to engage and destroy any target. He claims that he once ran into fire from the flank from seven 17 pdr A/Tk guns at close range and, having turned the hull of his tank so that a three quarter view was presented to the fire; proceeded to destroy five out of seven A/Tk guns with HE rounds. Several hits were registered on the frontal armour of the flaking from shell splinters.

The only situation in which he felt uncomfortable was to receive A/Tk gun fire from the flank and, having engaged the gun after having turned his AFV into the optimum position, to receive fire at right angles from an undetected A/Tk position in his rear. His reaction would then be to swing his turret as fast as possible and engage the more dangerous of the two targets.

The only time when a General Sherman stands a chance of knocking out a Tiger (in his opinion) is when it can close to less than 800 metres. He has observed that, even granted great superiority in numbers, Sherman tank crews do not venture willingly to close in, even on sides away from the principal preoccupation of the Tiger's fire. He claims that 3 Sqn has accounted for 63 Shermans since arrival in this theatre, 17 of which fall to his account.

The general opinion of the Sherman for its class was high. PW was instrumental in capturing two on the beachhead (one with a radial engine and one with twin Diesel engines) and the Bn had ample time to acquaint itself with these AFVs before removing the turrets and passing them back to 4 (workshops) Sqn for use as recovery vehicles, less turrets. His biggest criticism of the Sherman is of the visibility afforded to the commander when his hatch is closed down. He regarded the periscope as extremely poor.

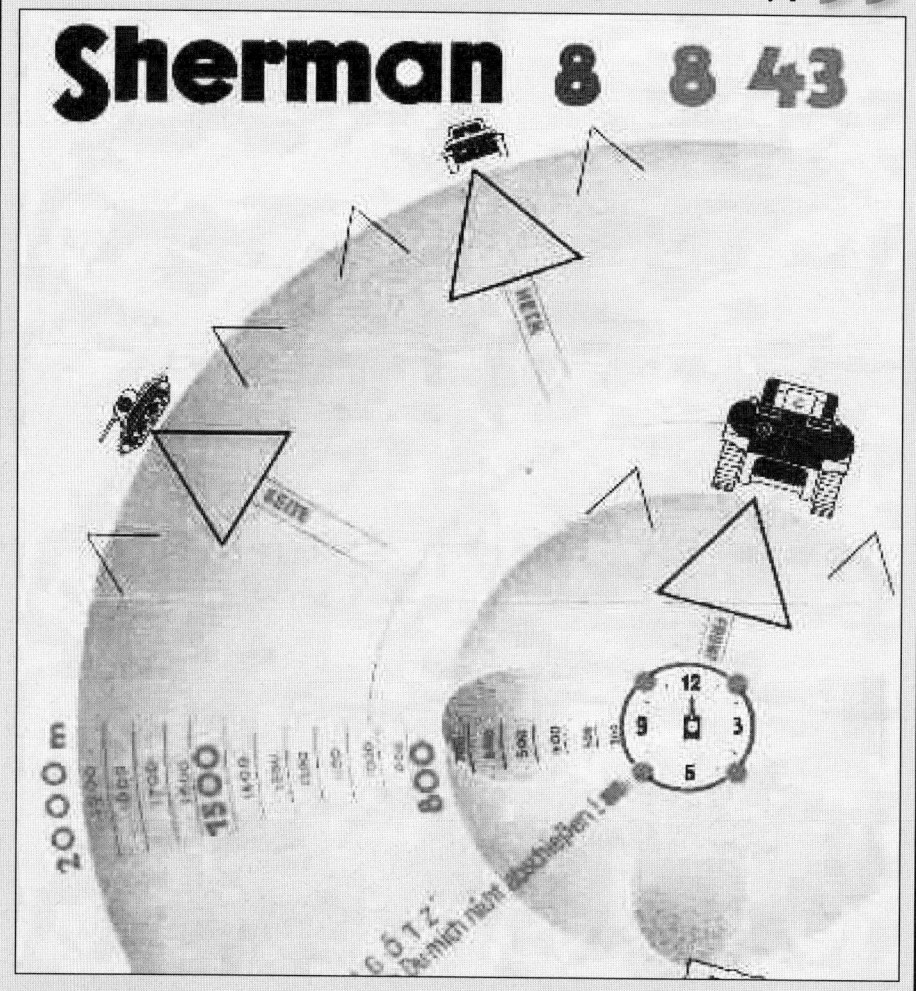

From Tigerfibel

"YANK" MAGAZINE

The following is an article on enemy vehicles tested at the Aberdeen Ordnance Research Centre from the January 21st, 1944 issue of Yank. The cover is an image of German Tiger I tank from the 1.Ko. of s.Pz.Abt. 504 which was captured by Allied forces in Tunisia.

The US Army did little to prepare for combat against the Tiger despite their assessment that the newly-encountered German tank was superior to their own. This conclusion was partly based on the correct estimate that the Tiger would be encountered in relatively small numbers. Later in the war, the Tiger could be penetrated at short range by tanks and tank destroyers equipped with the 76mm gun M1 when firing HVAP rounds, and at long range with the M2/M3 90mm AA/AT gun firing HVAP, and the M36 tank destroyer and M26 Pershing by the end of the war.

A Tiger I laden with grenadiers moves up towards the front during January 1944.

THE CONTEMPORARY VIEW NO.21
ENEMY VEHICLES FROM YANK

"At Aberdeen's Ordnance Research Centre, inquisitive experts finds what makes an Axis vehicle tick, and their tests produce facts worth remembering.

By Sgt. MACK MORRISS and Sgt. RALPH STEIN,
YANK Staff Correspondents

ABERDEEN, MD.

The first thing you learn at the Foreign Material outfit here is never, ever, to call a Nazi tank a "Mark Six" or a "Mark Four." The correct designation is Pz. Kw. VI or Pz. Kw. IV. "Mark" is a British way of saying model, whereas Pz. Kw. means what it says: Panzer Kampfwagen, or armoured battlewagon.

This extract is taken from Yank magazine

For more than a year captured enemy vehicles have been arriving here from every battle front on earth. The first was a half-track prime mover that came in sections and required three months of trial-and-error tinkering to be completely reconstructed. Missing parts, which were requisitioned from North Africa, never arrived; mechanics in the Base Shop section made their own.

The worst headache for repair crews here is the difference in measurement caused by the European metric system. Nothing manufactured in the U.S. will fit anything in a Nazi machine unless it is made to fit. In reconstructing the captured stuff, it has sometimes been necessary to combine the salvaged parts of two or three vehicles in order to put one in running order. The mechanics have made their own pistons or recut foreign pistons to take American piston rings; they've cut new gears; they've had to retap holes so that American screws will fit them.

Specially assigned recovery crews, ordnance men trained to know and work with enemy material, roam the battlefields of the world to collect the captured rolling stock, which is being accumulated here. It arrives with

Changing the huge front sprocket on the Tiger I was a regular job as the sprocket itself was set too low to the ground without much clearance and as a result was frequently damaged by obstacles.

the dust of its respective theatre still on it, plus the names and addresses of GIs who scratch "Bizerte" or "Attu" or "Buna Mission" in big letters on the paint.

Generally speaking, ordnance experts here have found German stuff exceptionally well made in its vital mechanisms, whereas the less essential parts are comparatively cheap. The motor of a Nazi personnel carrier, for example, is a well-built affair, while the body of the vehicle is little more than scrap tin. Japanese pieces of equipment for the most part are cheap imitations of American or British counterparts.

The engineers, who judge by the mass of detail employed in all German-built machines, are convinced that the Nazi idea has been to sacrifice speed for over-all performance and manoeuvrability. The German equipment, from the sleek motorcycle to the massive Pz. Kw. VI, is rugged.

The famous Tiger is the largest and heaviest German tank. Weighing 61 1/2 tons, it is propelled at a speed of from 15 to 18 miles an hour by a 600-to-650 horsepower Maybach V-12 cylinder engine. Maybach engines are used in many of the Nazi Panzer wagonen and in submarines. The Pz. Kw. VI has an armour thickness which ranges from 3 1/4 to 4 inches. An additional slab of steel mounted in conjunction with its 88mm forms frontal armour for the turret. Besides the long-barreled 88, it carries two MG34 (Model 1934) machine guns. Largest tank used in combat by any nation today, the Tiger is more than 20 feet long, about 11 3/4 feet wide and 9 3/4 feet high. It has a crew of five."

Tigers training in perfect conditions in Normandy during May 1944.

The reconnaissance element of a Tiger company had an equally difficult and dangerous job. This evocative study was taken in Russia during March 1944.

A Tiger rolls through a Sicilian town in July 1943. These machines had been destined to serve with the Afrika Korps but arrived too late to take part in the campaign. All but one of the 17 Tigers deployed in Sicily were lost in action.

TIGER I TANKS IN SICILY

In total 17 Tiger I tanks from schwere Panzer Abteilung 504 (s.Pz.Abt. 504) fought in Sicily in 1943 against the Allied invasion forces. All but one were lost in combat in the period from July 11th to August 10th 1943 when the German forces were finally forced to withdraw.

When the first elements of s.Pz.Abt. 504 with 20 Tiger I were sent to North Africa, the 2nd Kompanie remained behind in Sicily with nine Tiger I tanks. As a result of the surrender of German forces in North Africa, the nine Tigers of s.Pz. Abt. 504 were never actually shipped to Tunisia, but stayed behind on Sicily where they were soon called into action to repel the Allied assault which took place in July 1943. Prior to the Allied invasion eight additional Tiger I were shipped to the unit arriving early in the summer. By the time of the Allied invasion of Sicily, s.Pz. Abt. 504 with 17 Tiger I was attached to the Panzer Division Hermann Göring.

During the ill fated attack on the Allied beachhead near Gela, s.Pz.Abt. 504 was heavily engaged and lost ten Tigers in just two days of fierce fighting between 11th July and 12th July. Further Tigers were lost in action or abandoned during July and August as German forces slowly retreated across the island. In August, the unit's last surviving Tiger I bearing the tactical number 222 from managed to escape from the wreckage and was ferried across the Straits of Messina to Italy.

The following is an article on German tank trends, Panzer tactics, and how to fight the German heavy tanks from the October 1944 issue of the *Intelligence Bulletin*. The article includes suggestions from the Soviet Artillery Journal on combating the Tiger tank.

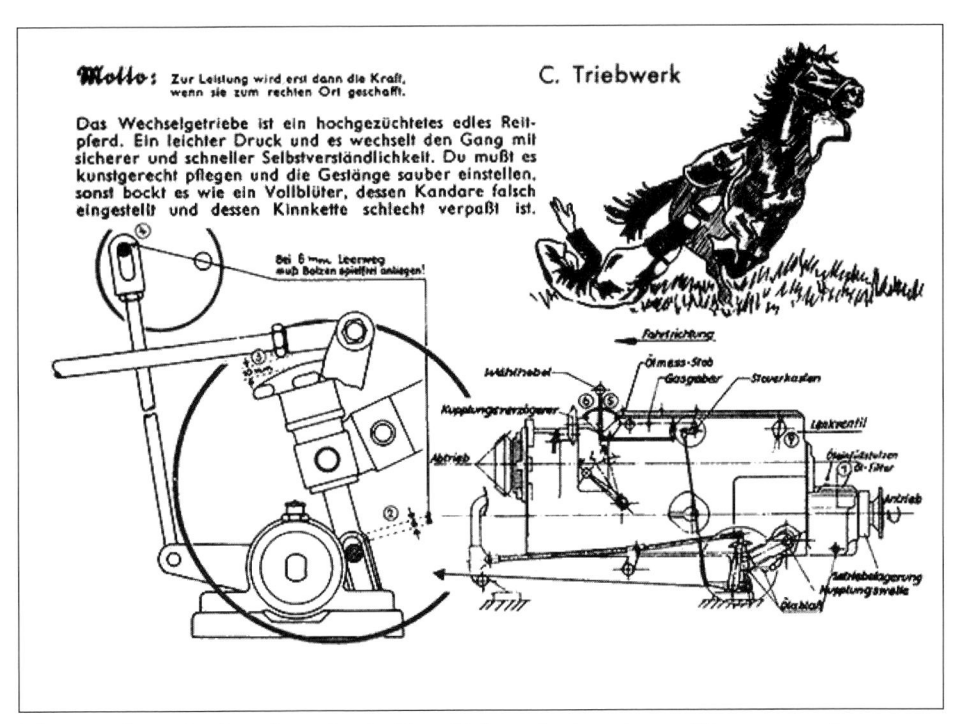

This page from the driver's section in Tigerfibel emphasizes the need for team work.

THE CONTEMPORARY VIEW NO.22
GERMAN TANK TRENDS

Officers plan the next move during a field conference in Normandy, June 1944.

"Just what can be expected from German tanks in the near future? Which models are most likely to be employed extensively? Are present models undergoing much alteration?

A brief summary of the German tank situation at the moment should serve to answer these and other pertinent questions.

There is good reason to believe that the German tanks which will be encountered most frequently in the near future will be the Pz. Kpfw. V (Panther), the Pz. Kpfw. VI (Tiger), and the Pz. Kpfw. IV. However, the Germans have a new 88mm (346-inch) tank gun, the Kw. K. 43, which is capable of an armour-piercing performance greatly superior to that of the 88mm Kw. K. 36. According to reliable information, the Kw. K. 43 is superseding the Kw. K. 36 as the main armament of the Tiger. A new heavy tank, which has been encountered on a small scale in northwestern France, also is armed with the Kw. K. 43. This new tank looks like a scaled-up

Panther, with the wide Tiger tracks. (Further information regarding this tank will appear in an early issue of the Intelligence Bulletin.)

During recent months both the Tiger and the Panther have been fitted with a slightly more powerful 690-horsepower engine in place of the 642-horsepower model. The principal benefit from this slight increase will be a better margin of power and improved engine life. The maximum speed will be increased by no more than 2 or 3 miles per hour.

Face-hardened armour, which was not used on the early Tiger tanks, has reappeared in certain plate of at least one Panther. On other Panthers which have been encountered, only machine-quality armour is used. There is no reason to believe that face-hardening would substantially improve the armour's resistance to penetration by the capped projectiles now in use against it.

It would not have been surprising if the Pz. Kpfw. IV had slowly disappeared from the picture as increased quantities of Panther tanks became available, but actually there was a sharp rise in the rate of production of Pz. Kpfw. IV's during 1943. Moreover, the, front armour of the Pz. Kpfw. IV has been reinforced from 50mm (1.97 inches) to 80mm (3.15 inches) by the bolting of additional armour to the nose and front vertical plates. And the 75mm (2.95-inch) tank gun, Kw. K. 40, has been lengthened by about 14 3/4 inches.

All these developments seem to indicate that the Pz. Kpfw. IV probably will be kept in service for many months. Recent organization evidence reflects this, certainly. In the autumn of 1943, evidence regarding provisional organization for the German tank regiment in the armoured division indicated that the aim was a ratio of approximately four Panther tanks for each Pz. Kpfw. IV. Now, however, the standard tank regiment has these two types in approximately equal numbers.

The possibility that Tiger production may have been discontinued has been considered. Although discontinuing the Tiger would relieve the pressure on German industry, it is believed that a sufficient number of these tanks to meet the needs of units equipped with them still is being produced.

Tiger tanks constitute an integral part of division tank regiments only in SS armoured divisions. However, armoured divisions of an army may receive an allotment of Tigers for special operations.

Early in 1944 a number of Pz. Kpfw. III's converted into flame-throwing tanks appeared in Italy. Nevertheless, it is believed that production of this tank ceased some time ago. Some of the firms which in the past produced Pz. Kpfw. III's now are making assault guns; others are believed to be turning out Panthers. It is extremely unlikely that production of Pz. Kpfw. III's as fighting tanks will ever be resumed, no matter how serious the German tank situation may become.

In an effort to combat attacks by tank hunters, the Germans have fitted the Tiger with S-mine dischargers, which are fired electrically from the interior of the tank. These dischargers are mounted on the turret, and are designed to project a shrapnel antipersonnel mine which bursts in the air a few yards away from the tank. Thus far these dischargers have been noted only on the Tiger, but the Germans quite possibly may decide to use them on still other tanks.

The Germans take additional precautions, as well. For protection against hollow-charge projectiles and the Soviet antitank rifle's armour-piercing bullet with a tungsten carbide core, they fit a skirting of mild steel plates, about 1/4- inch thick, on the sides of the hull. In the case of the Pz. Kpfw. IV, the skirting is suitably spaced from the sides and also from the rear of the turret. Finally, the skirting plates, as well as the hulls and turrets of the tanks themselves, are, coated with a sufficient thickness of non-magnetic plaster to prevent magnetic demolition charges from adhering to the metal underneath.

Despite the recent introduction of the new heavy tank which resembles the Panther and mounts a Kw. K. 43, it is believed that circumstances will force the Germans to concentrate on the manufacture and improvement of current types, particularly the Pz. Kpfw. IV and the familiar version of the Panther.

Evidence suggests that a modified Pz. Kpfw. II will shortly appear as a reconnaissance vehicle. Official German documents sometimes refer to it as an armoured car and sometimes as a tank.

ARMOUR AND ARMAMENT

The overwhelming advantage of the Tiger I lay in the quality of its main armament. From a 30 degree angle depending on the wind and weather conditions the Tiger's 88mm gun was capable of penetrating the well sloped front glacis plate of an American M4 Sherman at ranges up to 2,100m (1.3 miles). The better armoured British Churchill IV became vulnerable at a closer range of 1,700m (1.1 mile), the hardy Soviet T-34 could be destroyed at 1,400m

A Tiger I rolls through the open countryside in Normandy in June 1944. The tank is obviously some distance from the combat zone as the crew have not taken any form of anti-aircraft precautions.

(0.87 mile), and the Soviet IS-2 could only be destroyed at ranges between 100 and 300m.

The Soviet T-34 equipped with the 76.2mm gun could not penetrate the Tiger frontally at any range, but could achieve a side penetration at approximately 500 m firing BR-350P APCR ammunition. The T34-85's 85mm gun could penetrate the front of a Tiger between 200 and 500 m (0.12 and 0.31 mi), the IS-2's 122mm gun could penetrate the front between 500 and 1,500 m (0.31 and 0.93 mi).

From a 30 degree angle of attack, the M4 Sherman's 75mm gun could not penetrate the Tiger frontally at any range, and actually needed to be within 100 m to achieve a side penetration shot against the 80mm upper hull superstructure. However, the British 17-pounder as used on the Sherman Firefly, firing its normal APCBC ammunition, could penetrate the front armour of the Tiger I out to 1000m. The US 76mm gun, if firing the APCBC M62 ammunition, could penetrate the Tiger side armour up to a range of 500m, and could penetrate the upper hull superstructure at ranges up to 200m. Using HVAP ammunition, which was in constant short supply and primarily issued to tank destroyers, frontal penetrations were possible at ranges of up to 500m. The M3 90mm cannon used in the late-war M36 Jackson, M26 Pershing, and M2 AA/AT mount could penetrate its front plate at a range of 1000 m, and from beyond 2000m when using HVAP.

As range decreases in combat, all guns can penetrate more armour. HEAT ammunition was the most effective round but this projectile was rare and in short supply. The great penetrating power of the Tiger's gun meant that it could destroy many of its opponents at ranges at which they could not respond. The issue which was compounding the Allied tank crew's problem was the superiority of German optics. This advantage increased the chances of a hit on the first shot and in tank to tank battles one shot was frequently all that mattered. In open terrain, this was a major tactical advantage as opposing tanks were often forced to change position in order to make a flanking attack in an attempt to knock out a Tiger.

THE CONTEMPORARY VIEW NO.23
GERMAN TANKS IN ACTION

"A German prisoner observes that the following are standard training principles in the German tank arm:

(1) Surprise.

(2) Prompt decisions and prompt execution of these decisions.

(3) The fullest possible exploitation of the terrain for firing. However, fields of fire come before cover.

(4) Do not fire while moving except when absolutely essential.

(5) Face the attacker head-on; do not offer a broadside target.

(6) When attacked by hostile tanks, concentrate solely on these.

(7) If surprised without hope of favourable defence, scatter and reassemble in favourable terrain. Try to draw the attacker into a position which will give you the advantage.

A section of Tiger's deploying for combat operations in Russia during January 1943. The vehicle on the left still has the cover on the muzzle break which suggests this tank is not anticipating being forced into combat.

(8) If smoke is to be used, keep wind direction in mind. A good procedure is to leave a few tanks in position as decoys, and, when the hostile force is approaching them, to direct a smoke screen toward the hostile force and blind it.

(9) If hostile tanks are sighted, German tanks should halt and prepare to engage them by surprise, holding fire as long as possible. The reaction of the hostile force must be estimated before the attack is launched.

A German Army document entitled "How the Tiger Can Aid the Infantry" contains a number of interesting points. The following are outstanding:

(1) The tank expert must have a chance to submit his opinion before any combined tank-infantry attack.

(2) If the ground will support a man standing on one leg and carrying another man on his shoulders, it will support a tank.

(3) When mud is very deep, corduroy roads must be built ahead of time. Since this requires manpower, material, and time, the work should be undertaken only near the point where the main effort is to be made.

(4) Tanks must be deployed to conduct their fire fight.

(5) The Tiger, built to fight tanks and antitank guns, must function as offensive weapon, even in the defence. This is its best means of defence against hostile tanks. Give it a chance to use its unique capabilities for fire and movement.

(6) The Tiger must keep moving. At the halt it is an easy target.

(7) The Tiger must not be used singly. (Obviously, this does not apply to the Tiger used as roving artillery in the defence. On numerous occasions the Germans have been using single Tigers for this purpose.) The more mass you can assemble, the greater your success will be. Protect your Tigers with infantry.

A Tiger which has received a coating of anti-magnetic Zimmermit coating designed to prevent the application of magnetic mines by tank hunting teams.

THE TWO EXTREMES

The Tiger I enjoyed some spectacular triumphs on the battlefield, but it also endured its fair share of ignominious set backs. These two contrasting combat reports demonstrate the two extremes of the Tiger I experience.

On 21st April 1943, a Tiger I of the 504th German heavy tank battalion, with turret number 131, was captured after being knocked out on a hill called Djebel Djaffa in Tunisia. A round from a Churchill tank of the British 48th Royal Tank Regiment hit the Tiger's gun barrel and ricocheted into its turret ring. The round jammed the turret traverse mechanism and wounded the commander. Although the vehicle was still in a driveable condition the crew flew into a panic and bailed out. The complete tank was captured by the British. The tank was repaired and displayed in Tunisia before being sent to England for a thorough inspection.

In complete contrast to the dismal performance of Tiger 131 the Tiger I commanded by Franz Staudegger enjoyed an amazing string of successes. On 7th July 1943, this single Tiger tank commanded by SS-Oberscharführer Franz Staudegger from the 2nd Platoon, 13th Panzer Company, 1st SS Division Leibstandarte SS Adolf Hitler engaged a group of about 50 T-34s around Psyolknee in the southern sector of the German thrust into the Soviet salient known as the Battle of Kursk. Staudegger used all his ammunition and claimed the destruction of 22 Soviet tanks, forcing the rest to retreat. For this amazing feat of arms he was understandably awarded the Knight's Cross.

The Tigerfibel emphasized the smooth ride of the Tiger I comparing it to a sports car.

THE CONTEMPORARY VIEW NO. 24
HOW TO FIGHT PANZERS: A GERMAN VIEW

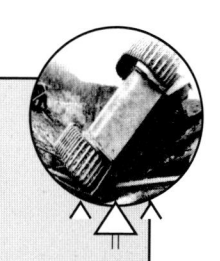

"

An anti-Nazi prisoner of war, discussing the various methods of combating German tanks, makes some useful comments. Although they are neither new nor startling, they are well worth studying since they are observations made by a tank man who fought the United Nations forces in Italy.

German tanks undoubtedly are formidable weapons against a soft-shelled opposition, but become a less difficult proposition when confronted with resolution combined with a knowledge not only of their potentialities but also of their weaknesses.

When dealing with German heavy tanks, your most effective weapon is your ability to keep still and wait for them to come within effective range. The next most important thing is to camouflage your position with the best available resources so that the German tanks won't spot you from any angle.

If these two factors are constantly kept in mind, the battle is half won. Movement of any kind is a mistake which certainly will betray you, yet I saw many instances of this self-betrayal by the British in Italy. Allow the enemy tank to approach as close as possible before engaging it — this is one of the fundamental secrets of antitank success. In Italy I often felt that the British opened fire on tanks much too soon. Their aim was good, but the ranges were too great, and the rounds failed to penetrate. My own case is a good illustration: if the opposition had held its fire for only a few moments longer, I should not be alive to tell this tale.

By letting the German tank approach as close as possible, you gain a big advantage. When it is on the move, it is bound to betray its presence from afar. Whereas you yourself can prepare to fire on it without giving your own position away. The tank will spot you only after you have fired your first round.

A tank in motion cannot fire effectively with its cannon; the gunner can place fire accurately only when the vehicle is stationary. Therefore, there is no need to be unduly nervous because an approaching tank swivels its turret this way and that. Every tank commander will do this in an attempt to upset his opponents' tank recognition. If the tank fires nothing but its machine guns, you can be pretty sure that you have not yet been spotted.

Consider the advantages of firing on a tank at close range:

(1) In most cases the leading tank is a reconnaissance vehicle. Survivors of the crew, when such a short distance away from you, have little chance of escape. This is a big advantage, inasmuch as they cannot rejoin their outfit and describe the location of your position to the main body.

(2) Another tank following its leader on a road cannot run you down. In order to bypass the leading tank, it has to slow down. Then, long before the gunner can place fire on you, you can destroy the tank and block the road effectively. Earlier in the war, a German tank man I knew destroyed 11 hostile tanks in one day by using this method.

Two Tigers pictured just before they were to go into combat at Villers Bocage in June 1944.

THE BRITISH RESPONSE

In contrast to the laissez-faire attitude of the Americans, who correctly assumed that there would never be enough Tigers in the field to present a potent threat, the more experienced British had observed the gradual increase in German AFV armour and firepower since 1940 and had anticipated the need for more powerful anti-tank guns. As a result of the lessons learned in France work on the Ordnance QF 17 pounder had begun in late 1940 and in 1942 100 early-production guns were rushed to North Africa to help counter the new Tiger threat. So great was the haste that they were sent before proper carriages had been designed and constructed, and the guns had to be mounted in the carriages designed for 25-pounder howitzers.

Hasty efforts were also made to get Cruiser tanks armed with 17 pounder guns into operation as soon as possible. The A30 Challenger was already at the prototype stage in 1942 and was pressed into service, but this tank was poorly protected, having a front hull thickness of only 64mm. It was unreliable, and was fielded in only limited numbers - only around 200 were ever built although crews liked it for its high speed. The Sherman Firefly, armed with the 17-pounder, was a notable success even though it was only intended to be a stopgap design. Fireflies were successfully used against Tigers. In one famous engagement, a single Firefly destroyed three Tigers in 12 minutes with five shots and as a result of the superior Allied product capability over 2,000 Fireflies were built during the war. Five different 17-pounder-armed British tanks and self-propelled guns saw combat during the war. These were the A30 Challenger, the A34 Comet, the Sherman Firefly, the 17-pounder SP Achilles and the 17-pounder SP Archer.

The gunner from Tigerfibel.

TIGER I TANKS IN NORMANDY

Something like 130 Tiger Is were deployed in Normandy during June and July 19944. The machines were chiefly deployed by the three schwere Panzer Abteilung equipped with Tiger I tanks which fought in Normandy against the Allied invasion forces. In addition, a small number of Tiger I tanks also fought in Normandy serving with the Panzer Lehr Division.

s.Pz.Abt. 503 was a particularly formidable unit and was transferred to Normandy with a full complement of 33 Tiger I and 12 of the new Tiger II tanks. The unit went into action in early July 1944. The 33 Tiger Is were all shipped to the unit in June 1944. Photographs of the unit's Tigers are very limited. Technical features are, of course, identical to late Tigers shipped to the other units. However one possible distinguishing features is the fact that spare tracks do not appear to have been mounted on front plate as was customary elsewhere. Camouflage patterning was similar to other units, but on at least some vehicles, the Balkankreuz appear to have been unusually large in size. Tactical numbers were relatively thin, neatly stencilled with a white outline and a very dark, probably black, interior.

s.SS-Pz.Abt. 101 received 45 Tiger I in deliveries in total beginning with 10 in October 1943, nine additional late model machines were delivered in January 1944, and 25 in April 1944. The unit reached Normandy in early June and Michael Wittmann and the 1st and 2nd Kompanie fought in the celebrated battle of Villers-Bocage on 13th June 1944. The Tigers issued to this unit included both the rubber-wheel and steel-wheel variants. Unlike s.Pz.Abt. 503 spare track appears to have been mounted on the front plate of most, but it seems not all of the unit's Tigers. Each Kompanie carried the distinctive unit marking of crossed keys in a shield, on the front and rear. In addition, the 1st Kompanie also carried a Panzer lozenge with an "S" and a small "1" on the front and rear plates. Tactical numbers were fairly large and dark with white outline, except for the command tanks.

s.SS-Pz.Abt. 102 was transferred to Normandy with a full complement of 45 Tiger I and went into action for the first time in early July. The unit was originally

A knocked out Tiger I of s.SS-PzAbt.101 lies abandoned in the ruins of Villers Bocage.

issued with a mere six Tiger I in April 1944 but received a further batch of 39 Tiger I in May 1944. Photographs of this unit's Tigers are very rare. However, the unit appears not to have mounted spare track on the front plate. Camouflage was large patches of colour which on some vehicles leads to the appearance of lines of the original dunkelgelb. Tactical numbers were thin, neatly stencilled with white outline and dark interior. Tactical numbers on the turret sides were often sloped, being aligned with the slope of the turret roof. Some Tigers carried a single underlined "S" rune painted on the zimmerit on the front and/or rear plates.

Panzer Lehr Division was issued 10 Tiger I in September-October 1943 and five Tiger II in February-March 1944. Of the ten Tiger I, three Tiger were listed as still with the division in summer 1944. The division reported six of eight Tigers operational on June 1 and three Tigers operational on July 1st.

THE CONTEMPORARY VIEW NO.25
VULNERABILITY OF THE PZ. KPFW. VI

A late model Tiger I lies abandoned after being knocked out in action.

"A tank is such a complicated weapon, with its many movable parts and its elaborate mechanism, that it is particularly valuable to know its points of greatest vulnerability. Recently the Soviet Artillery Journal published a number of practical suggestions, based on extensive combat experience, regarding the vulnerability of the Tiger.

All weapons now used for destroying German tanks - antitank guns and rifles, caliber .50 heavy machine guns, antitank grenades, and Molotov cocktails - are effective against the Pz. Kpfw. VI.

(1) Suspension System - The mobility of tanks depends upon the proper functioning of the suspension parts: the sprocket (small driving wheel), the idler (small wheel in the rear), the wheels, and the tracks. All these

parts are vulnerable to shells of all calibres. The sprocket is especially vulnerable.

Fire armour-piercing shells and high-explosive shells at the sprocket, idler, and tracks.

Fire at the wheels with high-explosive shells. Use antitank grenades, antitank mines, and movable antitank mines against the suspension parts. Attach three or four mines to a board. Place the board wherever tanks are expected to pass. Camouflage the board and yourself. As a tank passes by, pull the board in the proper direction and place it under the track of the tank.

(A German source states that this method was successfully used on roads and road crossings in Russia, and that it still is taught in tank combat courses for infantry. The mine is called the Scharniermine (pivot mine). It consists of a stout length of board, 8 inches wide by 2 inches thick, and cut to a length dependent on the width of the road to be blocked. A hole is bored at one end, through which a spike or bayonet can be driven into the ground, thus providing a pivot for the board. A hook is fastened to the other end of the board, and a rope is tied to the hook, as shown in Figure 3. Tellermines are secured to the top of the board.

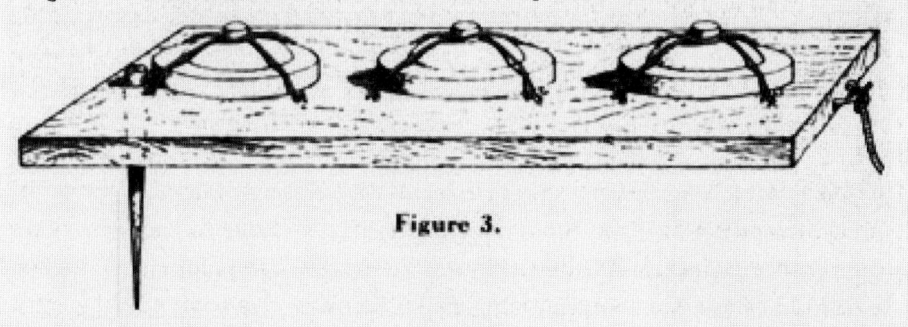

Figure 3.

One man can operate this mine. After the board has been fastened down at one end with the spike (in emergencies, a bayonet) and a rope tied to the hook at the other end, the board is laid along the side of the road. On the opposite side of the road, a man is posted in a narrow slit trench. He holds the other end of the rope. When a tank approaches, the tank hunter waits until it is close enough to the pivoted board, and, at the very last moment, he pulls the free end of the board across the road. The rope and slit trench must be well camouflaged. A good deal of emphasis is placed on this point.)

(2) Side Armour Plates - There are two armour plates on each side of the tank. The lower plate is partly covered by the wheels. This plate protects the engine and the gasoline tanks, which are located in the rear of the hull — directly beyond and over the two rear wheels. Ammunition is kept in special compartments along the sides of the tank. These compartments are protected by the upper armour plate.

Fire armour-piercing shells from 76, 57, and 45mm guns at the upper and lower armour plate. When the gas tanks or ammunition compartments are hit, the vehicle will be set on fire.

(3) Rear Armour Plate - The rear armour plate protects the engine, the gasoline tank, and the radiators.

Use antitank guns. Aim at the rear armour plate. When the engine or the gasoline tanks are hit, the tank will halt and will begin to burn.

(4) Peepholes, Vision Ports, and Slits - The main turret has two openings for firing small-arms weapons, and two vision ports. The turret has five observation slits. There are two sighting devices on the roof of the front part of the tank - one for the driver, the other for the gunner. There is also a port with sliding covers in the front armour plate.

Use all available weapons for firing at the peepholes, observation ports, vision slits, and the ports for small-arms weapons.

5. Turrets - The commander's turret is an important and vulnerable target.

Fire high-explosive and armour-piercing shells of all calibres at the commander's turret. Throw antitank grenades and incendiary bottles after the turret has been damaged.

The tank commander, the turret commander, and the gunner ride in the turret. The tank gun and many mechanical devices are found in the turret.

Fire at the turret with 76, 57, and 45mm shells at ranges of 500 yards or less.

(6) Tank Armament - The turret is armed with a gun and a machine gun mounted coaxially. Another machine gun is found in the front part of the

hull. It protrudes through the front armour plate, on a ball mount, and is manned by, the radio operator.

Concentrate the fire of all weapons on the armament of the tank. Fire with antitank rifles at the ball mount of the hull machine gun.

(7) Air Vents and Ventilators - The air vents and the ventilators are found under the slit-shaped perforations of the roof of the hull, directly behind the turret. Another air vent is located in the front part of the roof, between the two observation ports used by the radio operator and the driver.

Use incendiary bottles and antitank grenades to damage the ventilating system.

(8) Tank Floor - When an antitank mine explodes under the tank, the floor of the tank is smashed, and the tank is knocked out of action.

(9) Base of Turret - There is a 10mm slit going all around the turret, between the base of the turret and the roof of the hull.

Fire at the base of the turret with heavy machine guns and antitank guns, to destroy the turret mechanism, and disrupt the field of fire. Fire with high-explosive shells at the base of the turret in order to wreck the roof of the hull and put the tank out of action.

The Tiger I that knocked out the first M26 Pershing in combat. The victorious Tiger then backed into a demolished building and became immobile. The crew then abandoned the tank which fell into Allied hands.

THE SOVIET RESPONSE

The initial Soviet response to the Tiger I was to order the restart of production of the 57mm ZiS-2 anti-tank gun. Production of this model had been halted in 1941 in favour of smaller and cheaper alternatives. The ZiS-2 which had better armour penetration than the 76mm F-34 tank gun which was then in use by most Red Army tanks, but it too proved to be all but inadequate when faced with the Tiger I.

A 2.52 firing APCR rounds could usually be relied upon to penetrate the Tiger's frontal armour. A small number of T-34s were fitted with a tank version of the ZiS-2, but the drawback was that as an anti-tank weapon the ZiS-2 could not fire a strong high-explosive round, thus making it an unsatisfactory tank gun. The Russians had no inhibitions about following the German lead and accordingly the 85mm 52-K anti-aircraft gun was modified for tank use. This gun was initially incorporated into the SU-85 self-propelled gun which was based on a T-34 chassis and saw action from August 1943. By the spring of 1944, the T-34/85 appeared, this up-gunned T-34 matched the SU-85's firepower, but had the additional advantage of mounting the gun with a much better HE firing capability in a revolving turret. The redundant SU-85 was replaced by the SU-100, mounting a 100mm D-10 tank gun which could penetrate 185mm of vertical armour plate at 1,000m, and was therefore able to defeat the Tiger's frontal armour at normal combat ranges.

In May 1943, the Red Army deployed the SU-152, replaced in 1944 by the ISU-152. These self-propelled guns both mounted the large, 152mm howitzer-gun. The SU-152 was intended to be a close-support gun for use against German fortifications rather than armour; but, both it and the later ISU-152 were found to be very effective against German heavy tanks, and were nicknamed Zveroboy which is commonly rendered as "beast killer" or "animal hunter". The 152mm armour-piercing shells weighed over 45 kilograms (99lb) and could penetrate a Tiger's frontal armour from 1,000 metres. Even the high-explosive rounds were powerful enough to cause significant damage to a tank. However, the size and weight of the ammunition meant both vehicles had a low rate of fire and each could carry only 20 rounds.

The tide was definitely turning against the Tiger I and the Tiger II was introduced as a replacement in mid 1944. In order to shore up the crumbling morale and maintain the sense of invincibility the German School of Tank Technology released re-assuring combat reports such as the detailed example opposite.

THE CONTEMPORARY VIEW NO.26
THE JOSEF STALIN

A column of German infantry captured during the destruction of Army Group Centre file past an intact Tiger I now also in the hands of the Russians.

The new Soviet heavy tank, 'Josef Stalin', has caused the German tank experts no little worry. It is, therefore, of interest that the following unconvincing description of a 'Tiger' versus 'Stalin' engagement is printed in the official 'Notes for Panzer Troops' of September 1944, presumably as an encouragement to the German tank arm.

A 'Tiger' squadron reports one of a number of engagements in which it knocked out 'Stalin' tanks.

The squadron had been given the task of counter-attacking an enemy penetration into a wood and exploiting success.

At 1215 hours the squadron moved off together with a rifle battalion. The squadron was formed to move in file by reason of the thick forest, bad visibility (50 yards) and narrow path. The Soviet infantry withdrew as soon as the 'Tigers' appeared. The A/tk guns which the enemy had brought up only three-quarters of an hour after initial penetration were quickly knocked out, partly by fire, partly by crushing.

The point troop having penetrated a further 2,000 yards in to the forest, the troop commander suddenly heard the sound of falling trees and observed, right ahead, the large muzzle brake of the 'Stalin'. E immediately ordered: 'AP-fixed sights-fire' but was hit at the same time by two rounds from a 4.7 cm A/tk gun which obscured his vision completely. Meanwhile the second tank in the troop had come up level with the troop commanders's tank. The latter, firing blind, was continuing the fire fight at a range of 35 yards and the 'Stalin' withdrew behind a hillock. The second 'Tiger' had in the meantime taken the lead and fired three rounds at the enemy tank. It was hit by a round from the enemy's 122mm tank gun on the hull below the wireless operator's seat but no penetration was effected, probably because the 'Tiger' was oblique to the enemy. The 'Stalin', however, had been hit in the gun by the 'Tiger's' last round and put out of action. A second 'Stalin' attempted to cover the first tank's withdrawal but was also hit by one of the leading 'Tigers' just below the gun and brewed up.

The rate of fire of the 'Stalin' was comparatively slow. The squadron commander has drawn the following conclusions from all the engagements his squadron has had with 'Stalin' tanks:

(1) Most 'Stalin' tanks will withdraw on encountering 'Tigers' without attempting to engage in a fire-fight.

(2) 'Stalin' tanks generally only open fire at ranges over 2,200 yards and then only if standing oblique to the target.

(3) Enemy crews tend to abandon tanks as soon as hit.

(4) The Russians make great efforts to prevent 'Stalin' tanks falling into our hands and particularly strive to recover or blow up such of them as have been immobilized.

(5) 'Stalin' tanks can be brewed up although penetration is by no means easy against the frontal armour at long ranges (another 'Tiger' battalion reports that 'Stalin' tanks can only be penetrated by 'Tigers frontally under 550 yards).

(6) 'Stalin' tanks should, wherever possible, be engaged in flanks or rear and destroyed by concentrated fire.

(7) 'Stalin' tanks should not be engaged under any circumstances by

'Tigers' in less than troop strength. To use single 'Tigers' is to invite their destruction.

(8) It is useful practice to follow up the first hit with AP on the 'Stalin' tank with HE, to continue blinding the occupants.

The Inspector-General of Panzer Troops (who is responsible for this official publication) commented as follows on the above remarks:

(1) These experiences agree with those of other 'Tiger' units and are correct.

(2) Reference para. (4), it would be desirable for the enemy to observe the same keenness in all our 'Tiger' crews. No 'Tiger' should ever be allowed to fall into the enemy's hands intact.

(3) Reference paras (5) and (6), faced as we are now with the 122mm tank gun and 57mm A/tk gun in Russia and the 92mm AA/Atk gun in Western Europe and Italy. 'Tigers' can no longer afford to ignore the principles practiced by normal tank formations.

This means, inter alia, that 'Tigers' can no longer show themselves on crests 'to have a look round' but must behave like other tanks – behaviour of this kind caused the destruction by 'Stalin' tanks of three 'Tigers' recently, all crews being killed with the exception of two men.

Marshal Georgy Zhukov inspecting a captured Tiger

> This battalion was surely not unacquainted with the basic principle of tank tactics that tanks should only cross crests in a body and by rapid bounds, covered by fire – or else detour round the crest. The legend of the 'thick hide', the 'invulnerability' and the 'safety' of the 'Tiger', which has sprung up in other arms of the service, as well as within the tank arm, must now be destroyed and dissipated.
>
> Hence, instruction in the usual principles of tank versus tank action becomes of specific importance to 'Tiger' units.
>
> (4) Reference para (7), though this train of thought is correct, 3 'Tigers' do not form a proper troop. Particularly with conditions as they are at the moment, circumstances may well arise where full troops will not be readily available. And it is precisely the tank versus tank action which is decided more by superior tactics than superior numbers. However it is still true to say that single tanks invite destruction.
>
> (5) It may be added that the 'Stalin' tank will not only be penetrated in flanks and rear by 'Tigers' and 'Panthers' but also by Pz. Kpfw. IV and assault guns.

TIGERS IN ITALY

Due to Allied air superiority, the Tigers in Normandy and France were frequently employed mainly in a static defensive role. This conserved fuel as the Tiger normally consumed huge amounts of petrol. It also kept the mechanical breakdowns to a minimum. In other theatres such as Italy, Allied air cover was less comprehensive and the Tigers still enjoyed some freedom of action. This was not always a good thing however.

Although the Tiger was a formidable design and recognized as being such in a number of allied studies although the high fuel consumption and frequent mechanical breakdowns occasionally rendered its battlefield performance all but worthless. This was certainly the case with the 508 schwere Abteilung in May 1944 which the British report of which from August 1944 makes sobering reading and further deflates the myth of the invincible Tiger.

THE CONTEMPORARY VIEW NO.27
TIGER TANK IN ACTION FIRST MAJOR REVERSE OF 3 SQN 508 HY TK BN

"As an illustration of the difficulties encountered in the employment of Tiger tanks it is interesting to reconstruct one of the two mobile engagements on a Sqn basis which the Bn fought in Italy, when it won a victory and yet lost almost all its tanks.

The action took place between 23 and 25 May 44 in the general area of Cisterna. 3 Sqn, which had brought down 14 Tiger tanks from France, lost two burnt out at the end of Feb 4 – one through carelessness on the part of the crew and another by Allied A/tk action. It had received four of the latest pattern AFVs during May 44 and was two tanks over war establishment strength on 23 May 44, i.e. 16 instead of 14.

The Sqn formed up behind a railway embankment between the Mussolini Canal and the level crossing at G 063299 and engaged troop concentrations with HE. It then crossed the embankment and put three AFVs out of action in the attempt (one with gearbox trouble and two with tracks riding over the sprocket teeth). The remaining thirteen crews had all to stop on open ground because the guns had dug into the earth as the tanks came down the embankment and needed pulling through.

The Allied troops were driven back about three kms and a number of Sherman tanks surprised and knocked out.

The first loss sustained in action was a Tiger which had one radiator destroyed by an artillery round and had to limp back towards Cori in stages.

Twelve Tigers were thus left in action during the night 23/24 May 44. On the morning of 24 May 44 a retreat was ordered to everyone's surprise and A/tk fire accounted for one Tiger (hit on the right reduction gear and subsequently blown up by its crew).

Eleven Tigers withdrew to the embankment and the OC Sqn ordered five to continue to hold the enemy whilst the six were to tow away the tree tanks which had failed to cross.

Four of the six towing tanks experienced gearbox trouble and the OC then ordered the three towed tanks to be destroyed and tow out of the five fighting tanks to assist in towing away the breakdowns.

These eight AFVs were got back to an assembly point near Cori, leaving four Tigers only in fighting order. Of these four, one was hit by A/Tk gun fire and two more experienced gearbox trouble (all three were blown up), so that only one runner was left.

Two converted Sherman tanks came down from Rome during the night 24/25 May 44 and extricated the one runner which had also become u/s meanwhile, by towing it in tandem along the railway tracks.

By 25 May 44, the situation had so deteriorated that it was manifestly impossible to get towing vehicles through and the OC ordered the blowing up of the nine Tigers which had reached the assembly area.

Although a good many of the crews had gone back to Rome with the one runner, the OC and about 45 men were left near Cori. They had to march back to Rome and came under fire several times in the process, arriving in an exhausted condition.

PW states categorically that this action had a profound effect upon the Sqn's morale and also decided against the mass use of Tiger tanks. Of sixteen AFVs put into action, not one would have been lost, had adequate recovery facilities been provided.

Although the OC Sqn's personal courage was not in doubt, it was generally thought that he had not appreciated the situation and had created the disaster by attempting to salvage the three AFVs that jibbed at the embankment. Had he not done so, he might have saved about ten out of the original sixteen.

'Penny wise, pound foolish' was the criticism made of him. 3 Sqn also took a poor view of the fact that almost at once a new troop was formed from tanks drawn from 1 and 2 Sqn crews put in, the former crews going back to their Sqn pools.

The citizens of the liberated French town of Marle clamber around this Tiger I which was abandoned in the main street.

TANK LOSSES

With such an important range of industries in operation the city of Kassel was targeted for destruction and was bombed around 40 times by the Allies during the course of the war. These unwelcome intrusions severely disrupted Tiger production. The most notable occasion took place in late 1943. During the night of October 22nd/23rd the RAF dropped an amazing 1800 tons of bombs which obviously causing severe damage at the Henschel facilities. In addition to the damage caused to the infrastructure of the factory itself and the local transport system the RAF bombers also killed or injuring a high proportion of its workforce.

Despite these set backs and the huge difficulties which had to be overcome Tiger production continued right up until almost the end of the war. The U.S. Third Army began the battle to capture Kassel on April 1st, 1945. The Henschel works continued working to the bitter end and, as US forces approached, the Henschel factory completed work on the final batch of 13 Tiger II tanks which were handed directly over from the factory to two companies of schwere Panzer-Abteilung 510 and 511. Three days later at 1200 hours on April 4th, 1945 the city was surrendered and Tiger tank production was ended forever.

Tank losses on the eastern front by year:

Year	German Losses	Russian Losses	Kill/Loss Ratio
1941	2,758	20,500	7.43
1942	2,648	15,000	5.66
1943	6,362	22,400	3.52
1944	6,434	16,900	2.63
1945	7,382	8,700	1.18
Total	25,584	83,500	3.26

NOTABLE VARIANTS

In Italy, a field version of a demolition carrier version of the Tiger I was built by maintenance crews in an effort to find a way to clear minefields. It is often misidentified as a Berge Tiger recovery vehicle. As many as three may have been built. It carried a demolition charge on a small crane mounted on the turret in lieu of the main gun. It was to move up to a minefield and drop the charge, back away, and then set the charge off to clear the minefield. There is no verification any were used in combat although such a vehicle would have been of great value at Kursk.

During 1942, anticipating orders for his version of the Tiger tank, Ferdinand Porsche had actually gone as far as to build 100 chassis based on his Tiger prototypes. On losing the contract, the Porsche vehicles were used as the basis for a new heavy assault gun/tank hunter. In the spring 1943, ninety-one hulls were converted into the Panzerjäger Tiger (P), also known as Ferdinand. After Hitler's

The Elefant was deployed in Russia and also saw action during the Warsaw uprising in 1943, and finally ended its career in Italy.

The Ferdinand or Elefant, shown here in Italy in 1944, actually performed far better in combat than is generally perceived.

orders of 1st and 27th February 1944, the Elefant.

The Ferdinand represents a fascinating glimpse into what the Tiger might have been the Tiger had Porsche won the competition for the Tiger contract. This heavily armoured tank destroyer variant utilised all of the remaining redundant chassis which Ferdinand Porsche had ordered to be produced in anticipation of receiving the order for the Tiger I. These vehicles were a scratch built solution introduced into combat in 1943. The Ferdinand has an unfair reputation as a complete failure and is widely held to have floundered then disappeared following an unsuccessful showing at Kursk where the poor performance has been ascribed as being due to the lack of a close defence machine gun. The reality is that the Ferdinand was a highly effective tank destroyer which performed very creditably in Russia and Italy. Mechanically the Ferdinand was to prove remarkably reliable and in many respects may actually have been a better machine than the Tiger I.

Among other factory variants of the Tiger I was the fearsome Jagdtiger which was one of the most formidable tank destroyers of the war however production was very low and only 160 machines were built. Also of note was the compact, armoured self-propelled rocket projector, today commonly known as Sturmtiger, only 16 of these machines built and when the first of these was captured by the Americans a great deal of attention was focused on this remarkably powerful weapon.

The Sturmtiger with its 15in howitzer protuding. This calibre was as great as many a battleship's big guns.

The end for the Tiger I came in May 1945, almost three years to the day from its birth.

More from the same series

Most books from the 'Hitler's War Machine' series are edited and endorsed by Emmy Award winning film maker and military historian Bob Carruthers, producer of Discovery Channel's Line of Fire and Weapons of War and BBC's Both Sides of the Line. Long experience and strong editorial control gives the military history enthusiast the ability to buy with confidence.

- Tiger I in Combat
- Tiger I Crew Manual
- Panzers at War 1939-1942
- Panzers at War 1943-1945
- Wolf Pack - the U boats
- Poland 1939
- Luftwaffe Combat Reports
- Sturmgeschütze
- German Artillery in Combat
- Panzer Combat Reports
- The Panther V in Combat
- German Tank Hunters
- The Afrika Korps in Combat
- Panzers I & II
- Panzer III
- Panzer IV

For more information visit www.pen-and-sword.co.uk